TALES FROM THE
NEW JERSEY DEVILS
LOCKER ROOM

TALES FROM THE
NEW JERSEY DEVILS
LOCKER ROOM

A COLLECTION OF THE GREATEST
DEVILS STORIES EVER TOLD

GLENN "CHICO" RESCH

WITH MIKE KERWICK

SPORTS
PUBLISHING

Sports Publishing books may be purchased in bulk at special discounts for sales promotion, corporate gifts, fund-raising, or educational purposes. Special editions can also be created to specifications. For details, contact the Special Sales Department, Sports Publishing, 307 West 36th Street, 11th Floor, New York, NY 10018 or sportspubbooks@skyhorsepublishing. com.

Sports Publishing® is a registered trademark of Skyhorse Publishing, Inc.®, a Delaware corporation.

Visit our website at www.sportspubbooks.com.

10 9 8 7 6 5 4 3 2 1

Library of Congress Cataloging-in-Publication Data is available on file.

Cover design by Tom Lau
Cover photo: AP Images

ISBN: 978-1-61321-958-4
Ebook ISBN: 978-1-61321-961-4

Printed in the United States of America

To John, Jackie, and the entire McMullen family, for bringing professional hockey to New Jersey and adding a warm, personal touch to the Devils experience.

—Chico Resch

To Mom, who did not yell when her little boy stomped on her old Beatles LPs, rolled cans across her kitchen floor, and told her he was going to be a sportswriter.
And to Dad, who taught me that a bowl of ice cream, like the human spirit, truly has no limits.

—Mike Kerwick

CONTENTS

ACKNOWLEDGMENTS

When?

Promise to write a book and you start hearing that question a lot. Hockey fans who endure an NHL lockout will want to know when your book will hit shelves. Friends who get wind of the project will want to know when they can get autographed copies.

Now that it's here, in your hands, there's a long list of people who deserve credit.

John Quinn of the *Philadelphia Inquirer,* former sports editor at the *Asbury Park Press,* initially gave the green light on this project. Eric Girard was kind in dispensing days off after New Jersey's 2003–04 season ended. Greig Henderson and Barbara Jaeger are two of the best people to work for in the newspaper business.

Dean Reinke pitched this idea to us during the 2003–04 season. Laura Podeschi and Jennine Crucet, two of the editors who worked on this book at Sports Publishing, were unfailingly patient as the puzzle came together.

Holly Resch is a talented artist. She provided all of the cartoons that appear in this book.

Mike Levine, Jeff Altstadter, Pete Albietz, Erica Luthman, and Dan Beam—past and present members of the New Jersey Devils communications department—routinely put together a great media guide. The 2003–04 guide was an invaluable resource during the writing process.

Wendy McCreary of the National Hockey League Alumni Association was a big help when it came to tracking down former Devils.

Jack Falla provided inspiration when it was desperately needed. Debbie Waldeyer and Tom Gulitti *(The Record),* Mike "Doc" Emrick and Stan Fischler (Fox Sports), Matt Loughlin (WFAN), John Hennessy, and Aaron Richardson did their best to keep this project under their hats while it was still a work in progress.

Our families supported us from day one. Thanks to Diane and Holly Resch; thanks to Michael, Eileen, Jeff, and Brooke Kerwick.

The Hoboken Public Library offered a quiet, air-conditioned sanctuary where a writer could hammer out page after page on a laptop.

But the lion's share of gratitude goes out to the players, coaches, scouts, executives, and others who took the time to return a phone call or sit down in the locker room and relay their stories. Every one offered something original, something interesting. We can't thank you enough.

INTRODUCTION

AFTER CALLING ME TO HIS SIDE, John McMullen steadied himself on my arm and walked me over to a wall on the far end of his room. "Let's see if you know your history," he said.

On the wall, McMullen had hung small black-and-white photos of United States presidents. Each photo was taken on the opening day of a Major League Baseball season. Each one had a shot of the president of the United States throwing out the first ball.

McMullen, former owner of the Houston Astros and the New Jersey Devils, wanted me to identify every president on his wall.

I stumbled through the first few. Chico rushed over to help, but by then I had discovered a trick. Most of the prints were in chronological order. If I didn't recognize a president's face, at least I could fake my way through it.

"Richard Nixon . . . Gerald Ford . . . Jimmy Carter . . ."

Once I hit Nixon, I was in the clear.

"Ronald Reagan . . . George Bush . . . Bill Clinton . . ."

That pleasant afternoon inside his Montclair home was the last time I talked to McMullen. He died on September 16, 2005. He was eighty-seven.

People like McMullen—people who were not only willing to talk about their time with the Devils, but who were also willing to open their lives to a loveable goalie and a young writer with a tape recorder—made this book a pleasure to write.

Detroit Red Wings head coach Dave Lewis invited us into his office at Joe Louis Arena. Mike Kitchen called the morning he was named head coach of the St. Louis Blues. Scott Gomez and Martin Brodeur, two of the best storytellers in the Devils locker room, offered memorable anecdotes. Tom McVie had us scribbling down notes as fast as we could and laughing hard while we waited for a flight at Newark Airport.

And Chico, one of the great guys in all of hockey, made it all come together.

I was four years old when the Devils moved to New Jersey, seventeen when they won their first Stanley Cup title, twenty-five when I began covering the team for the *Asbury Park Press.* Most of the stories on the pages that follow happened long before I took my first cautious steps into the Devils' red-carpeted locker room as a sportswriter.

Chico was there from the beginning, first as a player, then as a broadcaster. If he didn't know the exact details of a story, he knew somebody who did.

There's a saying in hockey that a team is only as good as its goalie. That's great news for this book: Chico's an all-star goalie and an even better person.

—Mike Kerwick
June 10, 2007

TALES FROM THE
NEW JERSEY DEVILS
LOCKER ROOM

1

OUR STORY BEGINS

THE STORY OF THE NEW JERSEY DEVILS does not begin at the Meadowlands, the old practice facility in Totowa, or at the offices of Dr. John McMullen.

It begins in a suburb of Denver. It begins on a sidewalk that leads out the back entrance of the old Colorado Rockies training facility. It begins in a trailer.

I knew we wouldn't be staying in Colorado long when I saw the trailer. The Rockies had been cutting corners, tightening their purse strings more and more with each passing day. The latest victim was our locker room at the training facility.

"Where's our dressing room?" one of the boys asked the first day that preseason.

"It's out the back door," came the reply.

Forty feet out, there it was: a square trailer home without wheels. The inside of the trailer had been gutted. We got changed in the kitchen, hung our coats in the living room, and stored hockey equipment in the bedroom.

While at training camp in Colorado, the Devils were scrutinized by more than just coaches. *Illustration courtesy of Holly Resch*

Cold days were the worst, because the showers were located in the main building, back by the rink. We'd wrap towels around our waists, then sprint the 40 feet from the trailer to the showers.

A week into training camp, we first noticed some people eyeballing us from the building next door. They held up signs, each sign carrying a number. I asked one of the clubhouse guys about it. He said some of the girls in the office next door would spend their lunch breaks rating us on a scale of one to 10.

As the team's goalie, I never saw a number higher than five on those signs. Most of the other guys were checking in with sevens, eights, or nines.

When did I realize our time in Colorado was short? Later that season, when they put wheels back on the trailer.

ROCKY MOUNTAIN LOW

Mike Kitchen was on that Colorado Rockies team with me. Kitch is one of the few guys who was a member of the franchise at all three stops—Kansas City, Colorado, and then New Jersey.

The team didn't win much in Kansas City. The team didn't win much in Colorado either. By the time the team arrived in Colorado, Kitch sensed patience was beginning to wear thin.

"The game plan gets thrown out the window when you don't win," Kitchen said. "You have to show a lot of patience."

Losses mounted. Crowds stayed away.

"The fan base in Colorado was pretty good," Kitchen said. "Naturally, it wasn't large enough. The 7,000 or 8,000 fans we did have were very vocal. They really supported the team. It's unfortunate we couldn't make a go of it there."

Kitch heard the same rumors I did. The franchise was on its way somewhere else.

COKE IS IT!

By the end of the season, we all sort of knew we'd be heading elsewhere. As the days ticked down toward the end of the season, I turned to my wife Diane and told her, "We better take our stuff home."

I had a little wooden trailer I could hook onto the back of our car, but it was missing a back door. Somehow I needed to find a way to lug all of my stuff home without having it slide out the back on some Midwestern highway.

I'm a fan of signs, especially vintage ones. Late that season, I found a large tin Coke sign. The second I saw it, I knew it would fit perfectly on the back of the trailer. After I loaded the trailer up and hooked it onto our car, I nailed the Coke sign onto the back of the trailer. Problem solved.

Well, solved until I showed up for our final game that afternoon. The boys there couldn't laugh hard enough. They saw me pull up with that monstrous Coca Cola sign, the type you'd hang on a wall. I still take heat for it.

Diane and I made it home with all of our stuff intact. I'm still waiting on the endorsement money from Coke.

BUYING THE TEAM

John McMullen was down in spring training with the Houston Astros, watching over the Major League Baseball team he already owned, when former New Jersey governor Brendan Byrne first threw the idea out at him.

"Look," Byrne told McMullen, "you ought to see if you can get a hockey team for New Jersey."

"And that was the first suggestion I'd ever heard of it," McMullen said. "And so that's where it all started."

John made a lot of money in the shipping business. In the Astros, he already owned one professional franchise. But Byrne piqued his interest just enough to explore the possibility of owning another.

At the time, his son Peter was working as a ski instructor in Utah. John sent him down to learn as much as he could about the Colorado Rockies, a hockey franchise that didn't seem very happy in the Rocky Mountains.

It didn't come easy. Colorado's ownership group wasn't sure if it should sell. Then the New York Rangers, New York Islanders, and Philadelphia Flyers all chimed in, demanding a slice of the pie if the Devils were to move in and infringe on their territory.

John eventually paid the ransom. And just like that, hockey was on its way to the Garden State.

"Once the idea was presented," McMullen said, "I thought it was a good idea to have a hockey team here. But it was very difficult. We had a terrible time."

CHARTER MEMBER

When the team first envisioned a move to New Jersey, the club began mailing out letters to local businesses. If you loaned the team some money up front, you'd be able to get first crack at season tickets for the inaugural season.

Ray Henry, a Devils fan who lived in Glen Rock before moving to Mantoloking, was working for Henry Brothers at the time. He received one of those letters and loved the concept.

"They sent us paperwork to get Gold Circle seats," Henry said. "We put up $2000—$1000 a seat—and you could be a charter member."

During the 2003–04 season, Ray was named the team's Seventh Man, an award given annually by each NHL club to one of its most ardent followers.

"There's no such thing as a bad game," Henry said. "Every game is different. What always bugs me with other people, they leave early and think they've seen the game. [Sometimes a game] isn't decided until the last few seconds. They think they know who won. They really didn't until they read the papers the next day."

A NAME AND A LOGO

Ballots went out everywhere, asking fans to vote on potential names for their new hockey franchise. "Soldiers" was one. "Sailors" was another.

The one that got just about every vote in New Jersey was "Devils." It's the one owner John McMullen liked best, but also the one that might spark the most controversy. Before he officially christened the team "Devils," John paid a visit to the Archbishop of Newark just to make sure he wouldn't be offending religious leaders.

"As long as it has no evil connotations," the Archbishop told McMullen, "I have no objection to it."

Now that they had a name, they needed a logo. John's wife, Jackie, played around with design after design, trying to find something fans would appreciate.

"Days," Jackie McMullen said. "Hours. I'm no artist."

Some kids mailed in a logo that had horns atop the letter *N*. Jackie took it one step further. She sketched out a facsimile of the interlocking *N* and *J* seen on New Jersey Transit buses. Then she threw the horns on the *N* and sent a tail swinging off the bottom of the *J*.

It's a great logo, the same one the Devils have worn throughout their existence.

2

LEAVING CZECHOSLOVAKIA

JAN LUDVIG WAS AN ORIGINAL DEVIL, one of the few players on the planet who can say he pulled on a New Jersey sweater during that first season.

His trip there wasn't easy. Jan left Czechoslovakia and spent a year in an Austrian refugee camp before arriving in the United States. Unlike most hockey players, Jan never tried using hockey as an excuse for why he wanted to head to North America.

"I was eighteen years old when I made that decision," Ludvig said. "I was leaving with the notion in my head that I might never be able to go back or see my parents. It was just the nature of Eastern bloc countries."

The Edmonton Oilers were the first to pick up on Jan. He'd played for Czech national teams, so when they learned he was stuck in that camp, they bailed him out and brought him up for an amateur tryout.

Jan didn't stick with the Oilers. He played a season of junior hockey in western Canada before the Devils contacted him.

The tryout went well, so New Jersey inked Jan to a contract. He spent five seasons with the Devils. His second season was his best, a 22-goal, 32-assist campaign that put him second on the team in scoring.

"I met a lot of good people who extended their hand," Ludvig said.

TWENTIETH-BEST PLAYER

Hector Marini was one of the last few additions to that first Devils team. Billy MacMillan, the club's first general manager and head coach, worked out a deal with Islanders general manager Bill Torrey to bring Hector aboard.

Hector found out about the trade during the final week of training camp. He got in just one practice with us that preseason. Then, like the rest of us, he jumped feet first into the fire—on the ice.

"They were picking up players that weren't wanted from others teams," Marini said. "The twenty-first, twenty-second, twenty-third, or twenty-fourth player. That's the type of player I was with the Islanders: the twentieth best player."

You'd think that a collection of unwanted players wouldn't do very well. You'd be right: We didn't do very well.

"The first couple of years I was there," Marini said, "oh my God. We'd go eighteen, nineteen games without winning. Billy MacMillan was saying, 'Guys, we're going to be making history here soon.'"

A CAST OF CHARACTERS

What a group we had that first season. Carol Vadnais would be dressed to the nines, rarely traveling anywhere without a cigar in his possession. He was near the end of his playing career, headed for a career in scouting.

There was Dave Hutchison, a guy who could hit a target the size of a dime with the end of his stick. He had one of the best spears I've ever seen when he took out Brian Propp in one game that season.

And I'll never forget the Kid Line: Jeff Larmer, Aaron Broten, and Paul Gagne all earning minutes as youngsters.

It was exciting. But some of the guys in that first locker room you'd never see in any locker room ever again.

THE FIRST GOAL

The historic puck is in Don Lever's basement somewhere, stuffed away in an old trunk. Donnie doesn't have a huge memorabilia collection: a few pucks here, a few jerseys there. But he made sure to hang onto that first puck, the one that put New Jersey on the scoreboard for the first time in team history.

"It's one of my fondest memories of New Jersey," Lever said.

Donnie was one of the older guys on a real young team during that 1982–83 season. He scored the team's first goal. He was the Devils' first captain. All around him, young pups were lacing up skates, tasting the National Hockey League for the first time.

"We woke up in a hurry," Lever said. "They decided to go young."

It wasn't a young guy who got the first goal, though. It was Donnie.

That first game remains a blur for most of the participants. The Pittsburgh Penguins were on the other side of the ice. Donnie doesn't remember much about that first goal, only that it was a shot from the high slot that made it over the end line.

Years later, long after Donnie had retired and the Devils had won three Stanley Cups, he liked to think that he was at least partially responsible for all the winning that followed.

"We like to say us old timers were kind of the foundation of that success," Lever said. "The cornerstone. We had to put up with the abuse for them."

FROM WINNING TO LOSING

Before Dave Hutchison arrived in New Jersey, he played for the Toronto Maple Leafs and the Chicago Blackhawks.

Those two teams not only won, but they won often. So it wasn't easy for Dave to accept the way that first Devils team began collecting losses as if they were prized baseball cards.

"We opened up in a tough division," Hutchison said. "A real tough division. We did a lot of losing."

There were a lot of former New York Islanders on those early Devils teams. Guys like Dave, who got used to winning and were suddenly thrust onto a team that didn't do much of that.

To make matters worse, Dave and New Jersey coach Billy MacMillan didn't exactly see eye to eye.

"I don't know how it all got going," Hutchison said. "It was ongoing. In the end, I found myself up in the press box. It's not much fun. I was not used to being up there."

"It was time to think about hanging 'em up," he added.

YOU CLOCKED *HIM?*

In his National Hockey League debut, Jan Ludvig hit someone he probably shouldn't have hit. Most of his teammates were a little surprised he survived to play his second NHL game.

The Devils were playing the Pittsburgh Penguins the night Jan got his start. It was a blur, the way debuts are for most guys, but he remembers the moment he clocked Pittsburgh's Paul Baxter.

"I thought I killed the poor guy," Ludvig said. "They carried him off the ice on a stretcher."

Jan didn't know Baxter's rep. Later on he would look at Baxter's career statistics and realize that maybe he popped the wrong guy.

Baxter played 472 games during his career. He spent 1,564 minutes in the penalty box.

"Some of the boys were showing me [the stats]," Ludvig said. "They said, 'See PIM? That's penalty minutes. When you see 200 or 300 [penalty minutes], stay away from that guy. Don't hit him.'"

Eventually, the Devils and Penguins crossed paths again. Jan was probably going to spend at least one shift on the ice when Baxter was out there.

"If I don't die today," Ludvig remembered thinking, "I'm never going to die."

Jan got off easy. Baxter never said anything and never came by for retribution.

"Then years later I saw him," Ludvig said. "We had a good laugh about it."

THE BEST PEPPERCORN STEAK

Carol Vadnais loved his cigars. He rarely ever waited until he got home to start puffing away.

"Win or lose," said Vadnais's teammate, Hector Marini, "a big stogie would come out. He'd light her up."

By the time Carol got to New Jersey, he'd logged minutes all over the country. He played for two Original Six teams: the Boston Bruins and the Montreal Canadiens. He'd also played for the Seals out in California.

Carol knew all the good spots to hit on the road. He'd often try to rope some of the younger guys to go out with him.

"We were headed to St. Louis," Marini said, "and Vad said, I'm gonna take you for the best peppercorn steak in St. Louis.'"

"OK," Marini told him, not wanting to argue. "OK."

They got to the place, but the food was far from good. Hector had to muscle his way through a tough meal.

"It was the worst steak I've ever had in my life," Marini said.

But there was Carol at the other end of the table, his plate clean, a cigar in his hand.

"I told him that was the last time I'd ever have peppercorn steak," Marini said.

TWO WORDS

Jan Ludvig was working with a two-word English vocabulary when he first immigrated to the United States back in 1980. He knew "hello." He knew "beer."

"That was a good start," Ludvig joked.

He started soaking up words every way he could, watching Road Runner and Mickey Mouse cartoons at home and listening to the boys going back and forth in the dressing room.

"The first couple years I thought I was on the wrong planet," Ludvig said. "I'd listen to all these words, look in the dictionary, and none of them were in there."

And when one of his coaches was talking to him, trying to impart some pearl of hockey wisdom on the newcomer, Jan simply bobbed his head up and down.

"I nodded yes," Ludvig said. "I nodded no. I tried to look important. I fooled some of them . . . barely."

CHAPTER 2

ANYBODY WANT A PUPPY?

Hockey players love dogs. It didn't take long for Jan Ludvig to find one of his own.

"When he first came to our team," said Hector Marini, "that guy couldn't put a fence together. He was right from Czechoslovakia."

According to Hector, not long after Jan arrived in Jersey, he rushed out and bought a Doberman Pinscher named Zorba.

One afternoon, Jan showed up in the locker room and told the boys his Zorba had a litter of puppies. He wanted to know if any of the players wanted one. "I was the only one who said, 'Yeah,'" Marini said.

Hector soon had a puppy of his own. He named his little guy Boss, after Mike Bossy, one of his former Islanders teammates.

Hector's first season in New Jersey worked out great. But he didn't play as much his second season. He spent most nights watching games from the press box. Usually Boss would be there watching with him.

"I'd put him in my winter jacket and bring him up to the press room," Hector said. *"[New York Post* hockey writer] Larry Brooks asked me, 'What, you've got your dog here?' Boss would be running around. Everybody would be looking at me."

Boss lived sixteen long years. He was still alive when the Devils won their first Stanley Cup in 1995.

THE OTHER NUMBERS 3

Only two players in Devils history have worn No. 3 on their backs since the team moved to New Jersey in 1982.

Most people remember Ken Daneyko. The other man: Dave Hutchison, the first guy to wear No. 3 for the Devils.

"It's a trivia question," Hutchison said. "Who's the only other guy? I'm the only one who seems to get the answer right."

As far as statistics go, Dave's numbers don't quite measure up to Kenny's. Kenny played 1,283 games in a New Jersey sweater. Dave played in just 32. He scored one goal, had four assists, and picked up 102 penalty minutes.

"I find that pretty neat," Hutchison said. "They're going to retire it. They're going to retire it quickly. [The Devils retired Daneyko's number in 2006.] I didn't do it much justice. But he sure did."

3

ARE WE LOST?

THE MOST EMBARRASSING MOMENT of my Devils career came when we were staying in Landover, Maryland, before a road game against the Washington Capitals. On game days, I'd try to sneak in a nap during the afternoon. I called down to the front desk for a wake-up call, but never got one.

When I woke up that afternoon, I glanced over at the clock. 5:05 p.m. I threw on some clothes and raced downstairs, but the bus was already gone. There weren't many cabs hanging around, and I started to panic.

Lucky for me, a young couple was standing in the lobby, wearing Washington Capitals sweaters. They were going to the game that night.

"We'll give you a ride, Chico," they told me.

Sure enough, we got lost. Completely lost. I made the guy stop for directions, and the directions didn't get us any closer to the arena.

Meanwhile the clock is ticking away: 5:30 p.m., 5:45 p.m. Soon it's 6, 6:15. We were supposed to be in the locker room by then.

When we finally got to the rink, sometime around 6:40 p.m., there was a traffic jam leading into the parking lot.

"Listen," I told the couple. "Thank you very much, I'll run from here."

It must have been three-quarters of a mile. I came running down the steps as my teammates were heading out for the national anthem. On the way out to the ice, I had to pass the Washington bench.

"Hey, glad you could make it," one guy said to me. "You thought tonight was going to be that easy, huh?" said another.

Our coach, Billy MacMillan, was not happy one bit. I was supposed to start that night, but he threw one of the backups between the pipes. I've never pulled for my goalie partner as hard as I did that night. We were leading after two periods, but the Caps rallied and won the game. I knew I was in trouble.

After the game, Billy didn't want to hear my excuses.

"Chico," MacMillan said. "That's gonna be $500."

It was probably the most expensive nap I've ever taken.

DEVILS-FLYERS

In the late 1990s, the Devils and Philadelphia Flyers became bitter rivals in the Eastern Conference Atlantic Division. Before there even was an Atlantic Division, the early Devils teams planted seeds for that rivalry.

Glen Cochrane, a bruiser who picked up 1,556 penalty minutes over a 10-year career, was on those early 1980s Philly teams. One night he crossed paths with New Jersey's Hector Marini.

"Poor Hector had to fight big Glen Cochrane," said former Devils captain Don Lever. "He had raccoon eyes [after the fight]."

In the locker room before one Devils-Flyers game, Tim Higgins walked into the shower room and threw baby powder all over his body. Guys were getting dressed when Higgins came lumbering around, pretending he was a ghost.

"Oh no!" Higgins yelled. "It's the Broad Street Bullies. I don't know if I can play tonight."

Timmy loved pranks. And that one had the team laughing, even before a big game against a team as good as the Flyers.

YOU DON'T HAVE TO PUT ON THE RED LIGHT

We weren't very good those first few seasons. And the fans let us hear it. Instead of "Down in front!" they'd yell, "Up in front!"

The story I like telling involves a speaking engagement I was scheduled to make at a church one Sunday morning. I was driving out on Route 80 with a set of directions, but not a keen sense of the area. I was glancing down at my sheet of directions when I heard a police siren in the distance.

I looked around. No other cars were within shouting distance. He was pulling me over.

"Hey buddy," the officer said, his voice as gruff as that of the toughest NHL forwards. "What are you doing?"

"I'm trying to find this church," I said. "Did I do something wrong?"

'You went through a red light."

I started groveling. I told him I'd just moved to Jersey, didn't know a whole lot of people. At that point, I began bracing for the ticket.

And then he recognized me. "Don't I know you?" he asked.

"I don't know. Who do you think I am?"

"Don't you play hockey?"

"Yup," I said.

"You're a goalie, right?"

"Yup."

"Chico Resch? Goalie for the New Jersey Devils?"

"Yup. That's me."

I never saw the punch line coming.

"I've seen you play goal," he told me. "And you, more than anybody else, knows what a red light looks like."

Turns out he was a New York Rangers fan. At least he let me off without a ticket.

HEY NOW, YOU'RE AN ALL-STAR

Hector Marini went from being a fourth-line winger to an all-star forward in the span of one season.

"I can remember going to play in New Jersey," Marini said. "Billy MacMillan was the first guy to greet me. He said, 'You're going to play a lot here.' Billy had coached me in Fort Worth in the Central League. He knew what I could do and what I couldn't do."

On the Islanders, Hector was overshadowed by some of their big guns: Mike Bossy, Denis Potvin, Bryan Trottier. New York was in the midst of winning four Stanley Cups. New Jersey was still in its infancy.

"I was pumped when I went to New Jersey," Marini said.

Pumped, because he was finally getting a chance to really go out there and skate, score goals, and contribute. Hector played so well during the first 60 games of that inaugural season, his former coach Al Arbour picked him for the all-star team.

"I've always been grateful to Al Arbour," Marini said.

In more of a starring role with New Jersey, Hector finished the regular season with 17 goals and 28 assists. He saw time on the Devils power play, scoring five of his 17 goals on the man advantage.

"The first 60 games were good on a personal level," Marini said. "As far as the team . . . oh my God, we were so bad that year."

"NEVER LOOKING FOR ANYTHING SPECIAL"

In 1983, the Devils scouting department located its go-to forward in the NHL Entry Draft. John MacLean had scored 47 goals and had 51 assists during a 66-game junior season in Oshawa, Ontario. Billy MacMillan and Marshall Johnston, two of the decision makers in the Devils front office, recognized the pop Johnny Mac could bring to the offense.

Only five players were taken before the Devils grabbed Johnny Mac with the sixth pick.

"They were never looking for anything special," MacLean said. "They were looking for you to play. [Most teams] don't really look for eighteen-year-olds to play."

Three games into his first season, Johnny offered a sign of what was coming. In Detroit, looking to help his team shake off an 0–2 start, he followed a shot to the net.

"Davey Cameron took the shot," MacLean said. "I came in and got the rebound. It was my first goal, the only point I got the whole year."

The Devils won 6–3 that night, but the rest of the season didn't go so smoothly. He was back playing junior hockey after just 23 games in New Jersey. It took another year of seasoning before he was ready to tango with the NHL's elite.

"Should I have been [up with New Jersey]?" MacLean said. "Maybe not. In the long run, it did help when I went back."

THE MICKEY MOUSE COMMENT

Wayne Gretzky doesn't put his foot in his mouth too often, but I'm sure he regrets ever taking his now-famous potshot at the Devils one year.

On November 19, 1983, Gretzky's Edmonton Oilers beat the Devils 13–4. Ronnie Low was in net that night for New Jersey, a team that fell to 2–18 after the loss.

Gretzky was young then, still a bit of a brash kid. He called the Devils a "Mickey Mouse organization." You can imagine the comment didn't play well in New Jersey.

"He'd never said anything off-color before," said former Devils coach Tom McVie. "He didn't say anything off-color after."

I guess you could say New Jersey eventually got the last laugh, three Stanley Cups later, after New Jersey beat the Anaheim Mighty Ducks, a team that was named after a Disney movie.

HOLDING DOWN TWO JOBS

Billy MacMillan had to wear two hats for those early Devils teams. When we got to New Jersey, Billy was named both coach and general manager. In retrospect, Billy thinks it may have been a little too much for one guy to handle.

"To be GM and coach," MacMillan said, "that was just deadly."

Billy dealt with it as best he could. "There are very few people who can do both," he added. "Maybe a Scotty Bowman."

We weren't very good back then. The team won just seventeen games in 1982–83, and lost twelve of its first thirteen to start the 1983–84 season. Billy was fired as coach on November 22, 1983, the same day he was fired as general manager.

"I thought I'd be gone from the coaching end of it," MacMillan said. "The other [firing] was a surprise."

Billy, the team's first coach and the team's first general manager, is no longer working in the National Hockey League. Only now and then does he glance at the newspaper to check how his former team is playing.

"They've certainly done great things," MacMillan said. "But it was rough at the beginning."

THIRD TIME'S THE CHARM

For five years, Tom McVie lived in Room 424 of a Holiday Inn up in Maine. His family lived out west. His kids were going to school. He'd be back home in June, July, and part of August. But by September, he'd be back in Room 424, coaching the Maine Mariners in the American Hockey League.

Not long after Wayne Gretzky called the Devils a "Mickey Mouse organization," McVie picked up his phone and found New Jersey owner Dr. John McMullen calling on the other end of the line. The Devils owner told McVie to pack his bags; he was flying him down to Jersey.

'You've got to come down here and get this thing straightened out," McMullen told McVie.

"I was dragging my feet on the thing," McVie said. McVie was worried he would be typecast as an expansion coach. He had been the head coach of the Washington Capitals when they first came into the National Hockey League. He'd also been there during the early seasons of the Winnipeg Jets.

"Two expansion teams?" McVie said. "[Most coaches would say] that's out of the question. Three? You'll end up in a mental institution."

McVie had a great respect for McMullen. The way McMullen offered the job, stroking McVie's ego a little, eventually had him sold.

"I sort of said, 'Well, I think I'm OK up here [in Maine],'" McVie said. "But I never heard it explained to me by anyone like Mr. Mac."

McVie broke down. He had wanted to say no, but he didn't. He came in and took over the young team. It would be months before McVie tried saying no to McMullen again.

FOR RALPH

Martin Brodeur used to routinely put up nine or ten shut-outs a season, but back then I would've settled for one or two. We faced a ton of shots those first few seasons in Jersey. I got my first one in a Devils sweater, my only one actually, on December 17, 1983. We were out in Minnesota playing the North Stars. Ralph Romano, the athletic director at the University of Minnesota-Duluth, had passed away the previous night. Ralph and I were pretty close, and I wanted to play well in his memory.

It was probably the only perfect game we ever played. I saw the puck better than I usually did. I didn't mishandle any pucks with my stick.

I remember Bob Hoffmeyer took a ten-minute penalty. He was falling and clubbed someone in the head on his way down. It left us shorthanded, but I was having a good night.

If memory serves, I saw 42 shots and stopped all 42 that night. It was 1–0 most of the way until we added an empty-net goal in the waning minutes of the third.

A perfect night. I just wish Ralph could have seen it.

FIRST IMPRESSIONS

As captain, Don Lever tried his best to make the young single guys feel at home. Ken Daneyko, John MacLean, Ronnie Low, and I spent time over Donnie's place, eating whatever was on the menu that night.

"They just showed up and ate everything," Lever said.

The franchise was still on training wheels back then, and those dinners helped all the guys get to know each other better. At his home, Donnie welcomed the camaraderie. At the rink, he began sizing up some of the young guys, trying to figure out which ones would put together lengthy National Hockey League careers. He liked what he saw in Ken Daneyko.

"Just the size of him," Lever said. "Even at eighteen years old, he had that nastiness about him."

And he liked John MacLean, too.

"If Johnny ever hit the net," Lever said, "he'd have 40 or 50 goals. It took him a couple years to get his shot below the crossbar."

Donnie turned out to be a pretty good judge of talent. Kenny played 1,283 games in the NHL, all with the Devils. Johnny Mac had an 18-year playing career and wound up as an assistant coach with the Devils team that won the 2003 Cup.

TWO PATHS

Even when they were still young guys, Ken Daneyko and John MacLean handled themselves in two completely different fashions. Both guys were struggling for Tom McVie the first season McVie was coaching the team. Kenny was coming off a leg injury.

"Johnny Mac is playing," McVie said, "but he's so uptight it looks like he's skating around with [Brendan] Byrne Arena on his back."

The team could not send the players to the minors. They would have to go back to their respective junior league teams. So McVie sat down with Devils general manager Max McNab.

"These two guys are the future of the franchise," McVie told McNab. "We can't have them playing here."

McVie broke the news to MacLean first. MacLean was ecstatic. He thanked McVie, grabbed his equipment, and if you believe McVie, he was "almost singing in the dressing room."

"It was almost like I had lifted Byrne Arena off his back," McVie said.

Then it was time to tell Kenny. McVie called him in, told him they'd decided to make a few changes, told him it wasn't going to help anybody if Kenny stayed up with New Jersey that season.

"Are you nuts?" Daneyko screamed at McVie. "I'm the best defenseman here!"

"He went kicking his feet," McVie said.

"I was pretty brash as a youngster," Daneyko said. "I wanted to play so bad. I let it be known."

McVie was right about one thing: those two were the future of the franchise. Both were with the team when the Devils finally won their first Cup in 1995.

ROCK CONCERT

Even with all the padding, players can still find it scary when fans get out of control.

The Detroit Red Wings came to our place back when Steve Yzerman was a rookie. We were up 3–1 late in the third period when a bottle whizzed right past my mask and exploded onto the ice. One of the officials skated over toward my crease.

"Do you know how close that came to you?" he asked.

I told him I could smell it as it zipped by my head. I thought for a minute, "We're at home, right? We're in the midst of a rare win. What's going on?"

Up in the cheap seats, I spotted two kids staring back at me. Neither one could have been more than twenty-three.

They were standing up there, flipping me the bird. I couldn't figure it out.

After the game, once I had showered, I came up with a theory. There was a rock concert the previous night, some heavy metal show at the Meadowlands. My best guess is that these guys passed out at the concert, and when they woke up, they were at a hockey game.

WRONG GUYS

During the 1983–84 season, the Devils had Jeff Larmer, Rocky Trottier, and Aaron Broten on the team's roster. Jeff's brother Steve played for the Chicago Blackhawks. Rocky's brother Bryan played for the New York Islanders. Aaron's brother Paul played for the Minnesota North Stars.

That Devils team wasn't good, winning just 17 games on the way to a 17–56–7 finish. Tom McVie remembers picking up a newspaper one day and having a little chuckle at something one of the writers had written.

"The guy comes out in the paper," McVie said, "and writes, I've finally found out what's wrong with the Devils. They've got the wrong Larmer, the wrong Trottier, and the wrong Broten.'"

Jeff, Rocky, and Aaron all had good careers. Steve, Bryan, and Paul may have been just a little bit better.

GARRY HOWATT, GUEST LINESMAN

Garry Howatt had some knee troubles during his first season in New Jersey. He had an operation on his knee during the 1983–84 season, an injury that limited him to forty-four games over two seasons with the Devils.

As Howatt inched closer toward a return to the lineup, he began coming to games. He made a trip up to Hartford with the club. He wasn't ready to play, but thought he might get the nod that night.

Howatt got the nod. Just not to play.

A blizzard was hammering New England that night. The game officials were coming from the heart of the blizzard, somewhere up near Boston. Opening face-off was approaching. One official and one linesman were still caught out in the snowstorm.

At some point, a member of the officiating staff ducked his head inside the New Jersey locker room. They needed two linesmen, and wanted to use one player from each team.

Mickey Volcari, a scratch for Hartford, was the Whalers' guest linesman. Howatt handled the role for the Devils.

"I was just waiting for a fight to break out so I could get in there and break it up," Howatt said.

Howatt still remembers what he wore that night: a visiting Hartford Whalers jersey. Nobody could find extra black-and-white officiating uniforms, so officials had Howatt and Volcari wear Hartford's old green jerseys.

About a period and a half into the contest, the real officials made it to the arena. Howatt's one-game stint as a linesman had come to an end.

"I guess that's in the record books," Howatt said. "It was a lot of fun. I would have rather been playing that night."

4

TOMMY'S BIBLE

TOM MCVIE RAN A TOUGH PRACTICE. On game days, McVie had the guys skating hard, refusing to let up even though his team might need something in reserve for that night.

"It was amazing," said former Devils captain Don Lever. "After forty-five minutes in the morning, you had nothing left."

Donnie also remembers the book McVie handed out to all his players at the beginning of the season. The boys used to call it "Tommy's Bible." The book sketched out set plays, power-play scenarios, and penalty kill units. Sprinkled throughout the book were quotes, tons from legendary Green Bay Packers coach Vince Lombardi.

"If you didn't have it at meetings," Lever said, "you could get in trouble."

To catch guys off guard, McVie would call surprise team meetings, just to see who was trying to skirt the rules and leave the book home.

One afternoon, McVie called one of those surprise meetings. And Mel Bridgman didn't have his book with him.

"I still remember Mel Bridgman tearing down the hotel, panicking that he didn't have that," Lever said.

Lucky for Bridgman, one of his kinder teammates lent him the book and Bridgman was able to find a photocopier at the hotel.

"It was a little bit of cheating," Lever said, "but he was smart enough to get it [copied]."

ALBUQUERQUE MCVIE

Tom McVie and his wife had lived in eighteen states and four different provinces during his time in the hockey world. When it came time to name his sons, McVie and his wife chose the name Dallas for one child, and Denver for another.

One of his good buddies gave him a hard time over that.

"Good thing you didn't play in Albuquerque," he said.

YOU COST US LEMIEUX!

When the Devils put Tom McVie in charge 20 games into the 1983–84 season, the team was struggling. We'd won just twice, and McVie was desperate to turn our fortunes around.

"Pittsburgh was 12 points ahead of us," McVie said. "I started giving my Vince Lombardi speeches."

We weren't winning a lot, but we were winning often enough to speed right past the Penguins in the Wales Conference standings. Who knew that those extra wins would cost New Jersey a chance to draft one of the greatest players in the history of the National Hockey League?

"I did a little too good," McVie said, "now that history's gone by."

Don Lever, the captain of the team back then, remembers the talks McVie would give us in the locker room.

"Tommy was giving us this speech about not wanting to be in last place," Lever said.

"We thought deep down, 'God, doesn't he want [Mario] Lemieux?' We can't go lose it on purpose, but he's giving a gung-ho Churchill speech."

The Devils still got a good player with the second overall pick, drafting Kirk Muller. Muller finished his Devils career with 185 goals and 335 assists. He just wasn't Lemieux, a wizard on skates who may go down as one of the two greatest players to ever hit the ice.

McVie half-joked that during that off-season not many of his scouts were on speaking terms with him.

The following fall, McVie was walking around the concourse at the Meadowlands. He felt the stares, and realized people were beginning to recognize him. "That's Tom McVie," he heard one guy say. "Tom McVie," chimed in another.

"I was sort of feeling good," McVie said. "People remembered me. I could feel the energy picking up."

And then he realized why so many people were pointing at him. The next person he overheard offered the answer.

"That's Tom McVie," the fan said. "That's the son of a [gun] who cost us Lemieux!"

LONG, LONG YEAR

If it had been 2003 and not the early eighties, Bruce Driver might have gone back to college for his senior season at the University of Wisconsin.

"They weren't the team they are today," Driver said. "I was able to get my foot in the door."

Brucey was on the 1984 Canadian Olympic team. He played against some of the top talents on the globe. You do

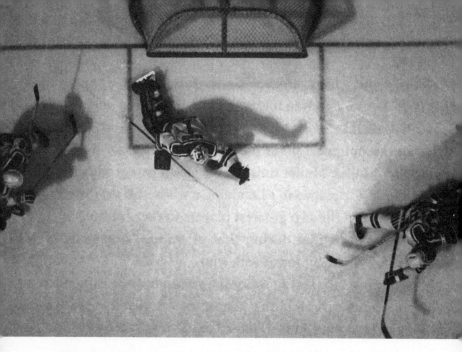

Glenn "Chico" Resch (1) stops the puck against the rival New York Rangers during the Devil's first season in New Jersey. *Focus on Sport/ Getty Images*

that, and suddenly playing for a young team in Jersey doesn't seem so hard. Twenty years later, Brucey calls that first stretch "the longest year I've ever had."

It began in June of 1983 with the Olympic trials, included a four-game stint with the Devils, and finally wrapped up when his Maine Mariners won the American Hockey League's Calder Cup.

How's this for an introduction? When the Devils first flew Brucey in, the New York Rangers were at the Meadowlands. It was the first Devils game he ever saw.

"I was blown away by the noise in the building," Driver said. "It wasn't Madison Square Garden, it was the Meadowlands, but it was still loud."

He made his NHL debut three nights later against Vancouver. Four games after Brucey joined the team, the Devils were eliminated from clinching a spot in the Stanley Cup playoffs. So New Jersey shipped him to its AHL affiliate in Maine, giving the young player more experience.

There was a good team there in Maine that season. Brucey's team beat Adirondack and Nova Scotia before stunning Rochester in the Calder Cup Finals.

"The newspapers had them sweeping us," Driver said. "We ended up beating them in five in that building."

It was a long year for Brucey, but one he'll never forget.

A POOR BUSINESSMAN

Tom McVie coached the final 60 games of the regular season during his first head-coaching stint in New Jersey, then decided it was time to ask Dr. John McMullen for an extension. McVie wanted a two-year deal.

At the time, the practice arena in Totowa had a satellite dish. McMullen liked to head there at night to watch his Houston Astros. Some nights, his wife would join him. The night McVie asked for the extension, McMullen was sitting there alone. McVie laid it out for him: he wanted a two-year contract, something that would give him a little stability, something his players would see and respect.

"I told him, if I work on a one-year contract," McVie said, "I'm almost like a lame duck guy. I said, 'You don't even have to give me a two-year contract. Just say you did so I'll have some clout.'"

"I really want you to stay here," McMullen said. 'You've done pretty good."

But a two-year contract? No way.

So McVie politely thanked him and turned toward the parking lot. He got halfway to his car when McMullen's deep voice bellowed, "Tommy."

"As I had my hand on the door," McVie said, "I stopped and said to myself, I've got him now. He's calling me back.'" McVie turned around to face the Devils owner.

"Tommy," McMullen said. "Let me ask you something. You're going to go back to the American League for exactly half the money? That's what I'm hearing?"

"Yes sir."

"You're going to travel all around to Halifax and other cities on buses instead of flying?"

"That's right."

"Instead of getting fifty or sixty dollars a day for meal money, you'll get thirty dollars?"

"Yes."

"Instead of staying in the Westin or the Drake you're going to stay at Motel 6?"

"Yeah."

McMullen shook his head in disbelief.

"I'm going to tell you something, Tommy," McMullen said. "You're a hell of a hockey man, but you're a piss-poor businessman."

McVie got in his car and drove off. He wound up in Maine that season, just like he promised.

"I thought because of the job I've done," McVie said, "I'll be down in Maine probably five or six months and I'll get a call from either Jersey or somebody. . . . Eight more years. Eight years, I ended up in the American League. Eight more years . . . and then I came back and coached the New Jersey Devils on less than a one-year contract."

DIFFERENT PATHS

Even as they came up through the amateur ranks as two hot young hockey commodities, Kirk Muller and Mario Lemieux never crossed paths. Kirk, the No. 2 overall pick in the 1984

NHL Entry Draft, doesn't remember playing a single shift against Mario, the No. 1 overall pick, until the two players arrived in the pros. But soon they were seeing a little too much of each other.

"Mario went to a weak team in the Patrick Division [Pittsburgh Penguins]," Muller said. "I go to Jersey. We played each other seven times [a season]."

What Kirk noticed was steady improvement from both teams. Using Mario as their centerpiece, the Penguins went on to win two Stanley Cups. Kirk had three 30-goal seasons in New Jersey. He helped guide the Devils toward their first playoff appearance.

"He has his style," Muller said. "I have my style."

Both styles worked.

A FOUNDATION

Yes, the team was losing, but Kirk Muller had reason to believe the losing wasn't going to go on forever.

"We were picking up a high draft pick [every season]," Muller said. "That's not only a key, but everyone was pretty much sticking. We were really gaining a good nucleus of a hockey team."

The Devils grabbed Ken Daneyko and Pat Verbeek in the 1982 NHL Entry Draft. They picked up John MacLean and Chris Terreri in '83, then Kirk in '84.

"It seemed to us that if we kept working," Muller said, "there was a light at the end of the tunnel. If you look at those years, each year we got stronger and stronger to the point where we made the playoffs the final game of [1987–88] in Chicago."

Looking back, Kirk thinks those early veterans, guys long forgotten once the team started winning Stanley Cups, helped give guys like him a major push.

"A lot of us at that age owe a lot to the older guys," Muller said. "Rich Preston, Don Lever, Dave Lewis, Mike Kitchen . . . all those guys. A lot of them are coaches and still associated with hockey. Those guys helped us begin."

I KNOW YOU!

First year, first game, and here were some familiar faces staring Kirk Muller down from across the ice. Kirk was playing on a line with Tim Higgins and Mel Bridgman, but it was the trio opposite him that had him nervous.

Ever hear of Bryan Trottier, Clark Gillies, and Mike Bossy?

"I thought, 'Uh-oh, this is a tough way to start in the league,'" Muller said.

At the time, there weren't many lines better. So here was Kirk and a bunch of kids going up against "the older, successful franchise," as Muller put it. "We were the new kids on the block, the feisty young kids," he added. "It was up to us to see if we could make this new franchise respectable."

That night, the Devils were respectable—more than respectable. They took it to the Islanders, winning 7–2 on the opening night of the 1984–85 season.

"It was a real surprise for us," Muller said. "I think the game was a blur. My family had flown in for my first NHL game. The whole night was obviously an exciting night for all of us."

One side note: Kirk's NHL debut also marked the first time New Jersey had ever beaten the Isles. If you can believe it, those Islanders teams from the early '80s beat the Devils the first fourteen times the two teams met.

And it was the first time in club history the team started the season 1–0.

MULLER'S FENDER BENDER

Kirk Muller got into a fender bender while driving around New Jersey during his rookie year. Little did he know his minor accident would make him easy prey for teammate Dave Lewis.

After the accident, Muller asked Lewis if he knew any good auto-body places where he could bring his car. Lewis knew a guy. So when the team went on an early-season road trip, Muller sent his car into the shop.

The bill wasn't too bad, something like $1,000. The auto-body guy fixed it, but didn't know how to get a hold of Muller. He wound up sending the bill to Lewis, asking him to pass it along to Muller.

A week went by, but Muller still hadn't paid the bill. Two weeks passed. Now the auto-body guy was calling Lewis, asking if he ever gave Muller the bill.

"He probably lost it," Lewis said.

Lewis and his wife were having some of the boys over for dinner that Thanksgiving. Muller was there. Craig Wolanin was there. Lewis also invited one of his other non-hockey pals, a private investigator.

That night, the investigator showed up with a fake subpoena and fake court papers. He said Muller was rumored to be traded to the Quebec Nordiques, and the auto-body guy wanted his thousand bucks before Muller left the country.

"Kirk was up in arms," Lewis said. "He called his agent. He called [Devils general manager] Max McNab."

Before Muller got McNab on the line, Lewis let him in on the prank. And not long after that, Muller paid the bill.

5

HAS ANYONE SEEN MY THUMB?

YOU DONT KNOW FRIGHTENING until you're out farming during the off-season and you accidentally slice the thumb off your left hand.

It was 1985, and Pat Verbeek was back home helping his dad out on the family's farm. Beeker, a professional hockey player with a gold mine of a future, accidentally chopped off his own thumb.

"At that particular time," Verbeek said, "it was very scary. My career was over in my mind."

Beeker rushed off to the hospital. His dad stayed at the farm, combing the ground for the missing section of his son's left thumb. The second he found it, he sped to the hospital.

Doctors took a vein out of Beeker's foot and transplanted it into his thumb. He spent two weeks in the hospital, but tried to keep the accident a secret from his teammates.

"The guys eventually found out," Verbeek said. "I didn't really tell anybody. I kept it to myself."

Within six weeks, his thumb had healed. And it didn't hurt his game at all. Beeker said the injury taught him patience.

The following season, he pumped in 25 goals for the Devils. He had 35 the season after that and 46 the season after that.

Beeker was New Jersey's first true goal scorer. Once doctors got his thumb back on, he was unstoppable.

BLINK AND IT'S GONE

The snapshot in his mind is still crisp. Craig Wolanin was ushered into the Devils family during the summer of 1985 with a press conference at the Meadowlands.

"I can remember standing there with Peter McNab," Wolanin said. "He says, 'Enjoy it. It goes fast.'"

Craig probably had a good chuckle over that one. He hadn't even played one game and here was some know-it-all telling him it goes fast.

Only years later did he realize how right Peter had been.

"Wow, that was an understatement," Wolanin said. "Before you know it, it's over. Blink your eyes and it's all gone."

Craig was only a seventeen-year-old kid when the Devils brought him aboard.

"I was quite nervous going into everything," Wolanin said. "But at the same time, I was full of optimism. It was almost like a spring day where you just feel like, 'Boom, let's get it going here.'"

He turned eighteen on July 27, then made his NHL debut during October. He is still one of the youngest players to ever don a Devils sweater.

"It seemed like I was finally able to reward my family," Wolanin said. "Especially my parents."

As rookies, David Hale and Paul Martin would learn during the 2003–04 season that first season is a blur and the hardest changes usually aren't between the boards.

"It's more difficult for a young athlete to adjust off the ice than on the ice," Wolanin said.

OH, PORTER?

Most rookies get pranks played on them during their first season. Craig Wolanin put one over on himself.

His first season in Jersey, Craig was living with Craig Billington in a hotel out by the team's practice facility in Totowa. He was there until Christmas Eve, while Devils management mulled over whether to keep Craig up with the team or send him back to his junior hockey club.

One day, after Craig had returned to the hotel following a morning practice, he spotted Doug Sulliman walking back over toward the practice rink. The team usually met there before embarking on a road trip. This trip was short, just two days, and Craig was about to start packing.

But Doug wasn't carrying anything. No suitcase. No extra clothes. Nothing.

"I knew it was an overnight trip," Wolanin said. "But I thought, 'Heck, he's a veteran.' So I didn't bring a toothbrush or anything, either."

When Craig got to the practice facility, he learned that Doug had actually brought his clothes over in the morning. Now Craig was hitting the road with only the clothes on his back.

"I pulled a prank on myself," Wolanin said.

Believe it or not, Craig was usually the guy in charge of luggage for road trips. Back in the 1980s, regulations at airports weren't as strict as they are now. Rather than waiting for a customer service representative to tag all the bags, Craig usually found himself counting up the pieces of luggage and affixing the labels himself.

"It was almost as if I was a porter," Wolanin said.

LEARNING THE ROADS

Mark Johnson grew up in the Midwest, far away from a metropolitan area like New York City. So when he first arrived at the team's practice facility in Totowa, he was hit by a wave of awe.

"It was eye-opening," Johnson said.

Mark joked that it took him a while to learn which way to go on the highways that weaved around North Jersey. But the trade-off was the Devils' travel schedule.

"Being on the East Coast," Johnson said, "travel is a lot easier. My dad was coaching in Calgary. The closest trip was Edmonton. They were flying quite a few places. We might be playing the Islanders, then Philly, then Washington. We'd be riding the bus. There were a lot of short trips."

In 2004, Mark was running the women's hockey program at the University of Wisconsin. Watching the Devils from afar, watching every Eastern Conference team for that matter, made Mark remember how much easier the road trips were in New Jersey.

"A bus ride or a short fifty-minute flight was a lot easier to deal with," Johnson said.

"I'M DONE"

Ken Daneyko was quite a physical specimen. He had to work hard as a hockey player, but building his physique was something that came a bit more naturally.

Craig Wolanin was Kenny's roommate on the road when the two were Devils teammates. One afternoon, Craig was in the weight room, sweating out rep after rep. A whole bunch of his teammates were doing the same.

Then Kenny strolled in. He had a towel wrapped around his waist. He was barefoot. And he was flexing, triggering a room full of laughter.

According to Craig, Kenny walked up to one of the weight benches and pretended as if he was going to start a set. He extended his hands, touched one weight, then backed off.

"OK," Daneyko announced. "I'm done."

The other guys were laughing, maybe even a little jealous.

"He worked hard and lasted a long time," Wolanin said. "A lot of [his physique] was God-given."

PAY AT THE PUMP

It was a two-hour flight, from take-off in Moscow to touchdown in Ufa. There were only eight or nine people on the plane, and David Conte, New Jersey's director of scouting, was one of them.

Conte was connecting through Moscow to take a peek at a prospect he heard about in Ufa.

Just before the plane was about to start its taxi down the runway, the pilot ducked his head into the main cabin. The plane didn't have enough fuel to make the trip, he told the passengers. He said the airline was issuing a $20 surcharge on top of the original fare, otherwise they weren't getting off the runway.

"It was like, 'Here's my credit card, fill 'er up,'" Conte said.

THE 334 CLUB

Without the Jeep, Jo Anne Lambert doubts they would have gone to the game that night. There was too much snow coming, and your average car wasn't going to have much luck out on the Jersey roads.

"I was the first one on the block to have one," Lambert said. "I looked for times I could throw it in four-wheel drive and drive."

On January 22, 1987, Jo Anne and Ray Henry got that chance. Ray had season tickets to the Devils ever since the team's move to New Jersey. There was no way they were going to miss the game.

On the drive to the Meadowlands from Glen Rock, Jo Anne and Ray saw one car after another pulled to the side of the road. What began as a light snow quickly turned into a blizzard.

"Buses stopped," Lambert remembers. "Cars stopped."

But their Jeep kept plugging away. When they finally pulled into the parking lot at the Meadowlands, there was hardly anyone else in the crowd.

"I suspect most of the fans thought the game was going to be called because of the weather," Lambert said. "We had a great time."

Several players from the Calgary Flames, realizing the game wasn't going to start anywhere near 7:30 p.m., came over by the boards to talk with the fans. They threw a few pucks into the crowd, maybe scribbled out a few autographs.

When the game finally got underway, hours after it was supposed to have started, the Devils began circulating a clipboard throughout the arena. Weeks later, Jo Anne and Ray were sent pins that pronounced them members of "The 334 Club."

That's 334, as in 334 fans showed up in an arena that seats 19,040. Some blizzard, huh?

After the game, Ray and Jo Anne actually helped a few of those stranded back to their cars. They met three or four hockey fans who were doing a tour of several arenas in the area and drove them back to their hotel.

Late that night, or you might say early the next morning, Jo Anne and Ray finally got home.

"A fun night," Lambert said. "I guess you would have to say the most unique, yeah. [We've gone to a] lot of Rangers games and had some bloodbaths in the stands. But that was certainly the most unique."

WE'VE GOT A GOALIE . . .
WE'VE GOT A LINE . . .

In the Midwest, Mark Johnson drove through snow all the time. He shoveled it. As a kid he played in it. He was used to snow.

The night of that blizzard, he was one of the first few Devils to show up at the rink for the 7:30 p.m. game.

"I was late," Johnson said. "I got there around 7:30, 7:40. What people were doing, they'd get stuck and instead of trying to get the car over to the side, they'd just leave the car in the middle of the road. No one could move."

The visiting Calgary Flames came out for at least two sets of warm-ups that night. They were staying at a hotel near the Meadowlands, so their players got there with no problem. But Devils players were coming from their homes, trying to navigate the roads and the cars stopped on them.

"It was before everyone had cell phones," said Devils forward Kirk Muller.

Mark was sitting in the locker room, watching a slow stream of teammates show up hours late for the action.

"OK, there's one more," Johnson said. "We've got a goalie. We've got a line. We can put guys together."

The game eventually got underway a few hours late. The Devils won, 7–5. Eventually the rest of Mark's teammates finished some of the longest commutes of their lives.

"Normally it took twenty to twenty-five minutes," Johnson said. "It ended up taking two hours to five hours."

PANDEMONIUM IN THE OFFICE

Fans who called Terry Farmer in ticket operations asked one question: "Is the game called?"

Players dialed into the office and told receptionist Jelsa Belotta "I'm stuck . . ." before finishing the sentence with "in my driveway," or "out on Route 3," or "just off Route 17."

Devils forward Peter McNab never made it by car. He left his automobile somewhere nearby and hoofed it the rest of the way.

When 5 p.m. rolled around, the snow was coming down pretty hard. Jill Polansky, one of the women in the office, tried to drive home. She was stuck on Paterson Plank Road for four hours.

The game got underway late that night, and Lou Lamoriello wanted to make sure the players had something to eat when the game ended. He sent Jelsa and Marie Carnevale in hockey operations over to the arena's restaurant and had them ask the chef if he could prepare a postgame meal.

"If you're going to need this, that, and the other thing," they were told, "you're going to have to help."

They helped fry up chicken. They washed dishes. You know, all the behind-the-scenes work you'd never find in their job descriptions.

By the end of the night, everyone—players, office staff, and fans—was exhausted. Outside the snow had subsided. Jelsa called her husband and said, "Come and get me."

"I didn't want to sleep on a trainer's table," she said. "I didn't want to sleep on a couch."

6

IS THAT PROPELLER SPINNING?

SOMEWHERE OVER THE HUDSON RIVER, on a short flight up to Quebec City, Aaron Broten glanced out his window.

There wasn't any turbulence. And Aaron never claimed to be an expert on aeronautics. But wasn't that right propeller supposed to be spinning when the plane was 20,000 or 30,000 feet above the ground?

On the left side of the airplane, players nodded off to sleep. On the right side of the airplane, players began wondering if something was wrong.

"I didn't even notice anything on the plane," Broten said. "It wasn't like we were veering into the river."

The pilot never made any announcement. He calmly turned the plane back toward Teterboro Airport, where the team disembarked before hopping on another plane bound for Canada.

"It was a little intense moment," Broten said. "But I guess it didn't matter. We could fly with one propeller."

I'M CAPTAIN?

If Kirk Muller was a little surprised to hear Devils head coach Doug Carpenter on the other end of his phone line, he was completely floored by what Carpenter was trying to tell him.

"He gave me the news that he would like to name me captain," Muller said.

On June 18, 1987, Kirk followed Don Lever and Mel Bridgman, becoming the third captain in New Jersey history.

"I got it at such a young age," Muller said. "It was kind of like leading the charge with a good group of friends around you."

GOOD QUESTIONS, BAD ANSWERS

Each spring, David Conte has to sort through all the questionnaires potential draft picks fill out before teams decide who to select in the Entry Draft. He's gotten some offbeat replies, to say the least.

"One of the questions was 'Who do you admire most?'" Conte said. "One kid's answer was The Silver Surfer, because he saved the world more than once.'"

According to Conte, the questions may seem silly, but the answers can be very telling. Conte once asked a potential pick what he would do with the money he earned if the Devils took him in the first round.

"He said he was going to buy a car," Conte said. "That's not a good answer."

Conte decided against selecting that kid one question later, when he followed up by asking, "What kind of car?"

"Well, I can't decide between a Porsche and a Corvette," he said. "So I'm probably going to buy them both."

Of all the prospects Conte has interviewed since he joined New Jersey's scouting department, few have offered better answers than those Brendan Shanahan came up with during a lunch meeting with his future employer shortly before the 1987 Entry Draft.

"The one question I asked him was, 'Why would you want to come to a team that's struggling?'" Conte said. "He looked at me like I had three heads. He said it wasn't a consideration. He just wanted to play."

Conte's follow-up: "Why you, Brendan?"

"Well when there's one potato left on the plate," Shanahan said, "my fork's in it."

"To this day," Conte said, "it's the best answer I've ever heard."

LUNCH WITH LOU

John McMullen first met Lou Lamoriello almost entirely by accident. John was supposed to have lunch with Tom Stevenson, one of his buddies from the shipping industry.

John wasn't exactly shopping around for a new general manager, and Lou wasn't exactly interviewing over lunch. Lou had been the athletic director at Providence College, but was willing to listen if a professional hockey franchise were to call.

After lunch, Stevenson put the bug in John's ear.

"You know," McMullen remembers Stevenson telling him, "you ought to think about this fellow."

Before long, John stripped Max McNab of his title as general manager and brought Lou aboard to give the franchise a new vision.

"I think the main thing he brought," said McMullen, "was that you could tell he was an honest individual."

Oleg Tverdovsky and Ken Daneyko celebrate New Jersey's 3-0 Victory over Anaheim in Game 7 of the 2003 Stanley Cup Finals. The win helped the Devils claim their third Stanley Cup title. *Elsa/NHLI/Getty Images*

It was a move that eventually made both John and Lou look brilliant. Later that season, John's team clinched a playoff berth for the first time in team history.

ACCEPTING LOSSES

The cleaning began the moment Lou Lamoriello arrived in New Jersey. He saw things he liked during his first few days in New Jersey, but he also saw several things he didn't like.

Taking a team that had never gone to the playoffs and turning it into an elite-level franchise was going to take some time. To get there, Lou wanted to rid the Meadowlands of what he felt was a culture of losing. In all his years as athletic director and hockey coach at Providence, Lou never had a stomach for losses.

In New Jersey, "Nobody believed they could win," Lamoriello said. "They accepted losing. They were satisfied with the work ethic."

He tried to find the source of that attitude. He didn't know if one losing season simply made the next one easier to swallow. He didn't know if it was because so many of the young guys knew nothing other than playing the role of underdog. "I couldn't put my finger on it," Lamoriello said of trying to dissect his team.

"If you were playing well and lost," Lamoriello said, "there was [still] a certain amount of satisfaction. But that wasn't the case, so it couldn't have been that."

New Jersey head coach Doug Carpenter became the first casualty. Lou liked the way Doug preached fundamentals, but didn't like the way Doug's players seemed content. On January 26, 1988, Lou moved Doug out and named Jim Schoenfeld the fourth head coach of the Devils.

"It got to a point where we could get to the playoffs," Lamoriello said. "Jimmy Schoenfeld did a great job of bringing life and enthusiasm and positivity."

FOUR-YEAR VETERANS

Brendan Shanahan remembers the difficulty of his rookie year: the travel, the schedule, the fights—it was all a blur.

Late in the 1987–88 season, Kirk Muller went up to Shanny, trying to reassure him that all rookies have a rough go of it.

"Your first year goes by slowly," Muller told Shanny. "Me, I'm in my fourth year. My career has flown by."

"I ate it up," Shanny said. "I thought, 'Four years, wow. He's been around the block.'"

Years later, Shanny would laugh at that. Four years in the Red Wings locker room, he said, and you'd still be buying rookie meals.

POOR DOUGIE

Whether it's carrying bags, or buying team meals, or falling into some trap laid out by a veteran, most rookies have to undergo some sort of initiation when they enter the league. In New Jersey, several rookies found the price of being a first-year player was the hair on their heads.

Brendan Shanahan and Doug Brown both came up as rookies during the 1987–88 season. Shanny was a great guy, a good team player. But there was no way the boys weren't going to shave his head. They'd have to get Dougie, too, even though he was getting married that summer and had tried his best to lobby his way out of it.

"Everyone felt bad for Doug Brown," said Devils defenseman Bruce Driver. "He was doing everything he could possibly do to not be initiated. 'I'll take everybody out for dinner. I'll take you guys out for dinner twice.'"

When it came time to buzz Dougie's head, they took pity on him.

"Fortunately for him, he did get out of it," Driver said.

The compromise? "We shaved the rest of his body," Driver said.

STAYING IN HOTELS . . . AT HOME

The tradition began in 1988, as the Devils stretched for every available inch of ground they could cover in the Wales Conference standings. With his team chasing its first-ever trip to the playoffs, New Jersey general manager Lou Lamoriello had his staff book hotel rooms for the players at a hotel near the Meadowlands.

I know, I know. It's one thing to stay in some of the ritziest hotels on the road, one of the fringe benefits accorded to professional athletes. But at home? Most outsiders thought the decision seemed a bit odd at the time.

"Odd at the time?" wondered former Devils forward John MacLean. "Or what we needed? It was a good idea. We had never been in that situation as a group. I think we were all looking for one of those things. No one complained."

Johnny Mac remembers a car service showing up at the hotel, carrying four or five players per trip to the rink.

It worked. And it's a tradition Lou revived on more than one occasion. During New Jersey's run to the 2003 Cup, the Devils spent nights before home games at a hotel near the Meadowlands.

BURKE'S WILD DEBUT

Letting six goals into your net normally means your postgame ritual will include hanging your head in shame and letting hot water rain over you in the locker-room shower.

So why was Sean Burke so happy after six pucks beat him on March 5, 1988? Because the guy at the other end of the ice, Boston's Reggie Lemelin, let seven pucks into his net.

"I battled right through," Burke said. "We won it in overtime."

It was a landmark win for Burkey; it was Burkey's first NHL start. He'd cracked the lineup for the first time only three days earlier, when New Jersey coach Jim Schoenfeld sent him in to mop up during the final period of a 6–1 loss to the Islanders. Schoenfeld had put him in for the full sixty minutes in the

Boston game. Burkey hadn't been great, but the Devils had walked away with the win.

Years later, Burkey ran into Reggie Lemelin.

"He joked about how it was one of the worst games he ever played," Burke said. "I said, 'It wasn't a great game for me either, but we won 7–6 in overtime.' It was an exciting start anyway."

Andy Brickley got the game-winner and suddenly Burkey had a regular spot in the lineup. He didn't get his first start until 68 games into the 80-game season, but then went 10–1 down the stretch as New Jersey made a run at the playoffs.

"We were in a playoff race but really we weren't in it," Burke said. "We had to basically win every game. There were still twelve or thirteen games left. We didn't really think that was the way things would play out."

With Burkey in net most of the way, New Jersey lost just twice over the club's final 13 games that season.

"It was exciting," Burke said. "There was just a lot of energy after winning that [Boston] game. It seemed to just build. It was a starting point."

7

OPENING DOORS

WHEN DID THAT FIRST PLAYOFF appearance seem attainable? It wasn't on one dramatic rush up ice or one dramatic save in net. It was in the hallway of a hotel on the road.

It was March, late in the 1987–88 season, and the Devils were on one of the team's final road trips. A bunch of the boys had the Rangers game on in their hotel rooms. By then, everybody knew there were three teams vying for the final playoff berth: the Rangers, the Devils, and the Pittsburgh Penguins.

The way New Jersey forward Pat Verbeek remembers it, the Rangers lost that night to a team that had no business beating them. "Everyone knew the schedule," said Verbeek. "Mathematically, [after a Rangers loss], if we took care of our side, we'd be in the playoffs. It was a pretty exciting moment."

Hotel room doors began swinging open. Players started cheering. There were smiles up and down the hall that night. "We were basically whooping it up," Verbeek said. "We knew we had a chance."

Beeker's Devils went 8–1–1 down the stretch, clinching the final playoff spot with a win in Chicago on the final day.

If the Rangers hadn't lost that game, maybe the Devils would have had to wait a few more seasons for their first playoff appearance. For a team that had never made the playoffs, another trip home would have been tough to stomach.

"You'd go home in the summertime, home early every year," Verbeek said. "I think that was kind of upsetting."

BEEKER'S PENALTY SHOT

On the biggest goal of his Devils career, Pat Verbeek's body wouldn't cooperate. The tension of a tight game with the New York Rangers had jangled his nerves, and one of his legs was twitching nonstop.

"I remember how bad my right leg was shaking," Verbeek said. "I was nervous, wanting to score. I couldn't get it to stop. I tried to keep skating so it would go away."

Beeker scored 170 goals during his seven-season tenure in New Jersey, none bigger than that penalty shot he nailed against the New York Rangers on March 27, 1988.

The Devils went up 2–1 against New York, but the Rangers were quickly building momentum. One strike, and the lead would vanish, taking New Jersey's playoff hopes with it.

Then the officials awarded Beeker a penalty shot, one of four New Jersey had that season. The officials sent him over for a one-on-one showdown with Rangers goalie John Vanbiesbrouck, a guy who later spent two seasons in New Jersey.

"It was a chance to really kill them, stick the nail in the coffin," Verbeek said.

"I wanted to go top shelf over the glove on Vanbiesbrouck. He didn't give it to me. I took Option 2. I took it to my backhand and roofed it."

Option 2 worked. Verbeek beat Vanbiesbrouck, and the Devils went on to beat the Rangers 7–2.

"The whole bench erupted," Verbeek said.

THE BIGGEST GOAL OF THE ERA

The bridge from one era of Devils hockey to another (and better) era of Devils hockey is only one goal in length.

Am I oversimplifying things? Maybe. But everything really changed for the franchise when John MacLean scored an overtime goal in Chicago, sending the Devils rollicking into the playoffs for the first time in team history.

New Jersey was actually trailing in the game, when Johnny Mac got his stick on the puck and tied things up. But to make the playoffs, the Devils needed a win, not a tie, and the players went back to the locker room at the end of regulation deadlocked with the Blackhawks at 3–3.

Sean Burke, green as those old Devils uniforms, stood up and reminded his teammates which side had the better group of players.

"Burkey was like, 'Come on. We're gonna win this thing,'" MacLean said. "I'm pretty sure he said, 'I'll do my job.'"

Burkey did his job. The weight fell on the offense's shoulders. Johnny Mac had already scored 22 goals during the first 79 games and three periods of that 1987–88 campaign. But his season would be incomplete without goal No. 23.

"Joe Cirella made a great play at the point," MacLean said. "He made a move on the D-man."

That was the opening.

"[Joe] put a wrister on net," MacLean said. "As he was shooting, I came off the wall and the rebound came right out to me. As soon as it hit my stick, I fired it back in."

He was surrounded, trampled, and exhilarated all at the same time.

The Devils won just 17 games during the 1982–83 season, and just 17 more the season after that. Now they were going to the playoffs.

"There had been lots of hard work before that finally happened," said Aaron Broten, a forward who scored 83 points that season. "For us to get in there was a load off the back of a lot of people who had been there half a dozen years."

CELEBRATION TIME

Before those three Stanley Cups, before the team emerged as a year-in, year-out threat to win it all, there was that first moment of magic.

"It felt like you'd just won the Stanley Cup Championship," Brendan Shanahan told me years later while standing in the middle of the Detroit Red Wings locker room.

Shanny was a Devils rookie back then, just nineteen years old when New Jersey clinched its first playoff berth in team history. He would go on to score 50 goals in back-to-back seasons with St. Louis and would later win three Cups with Detroit.

That first season, the 1987–88 campaign, Shanny was a fourth-liner who piled up 131 penalty minutes and scored just seven goals.

What he remembers most was the celebration. He was one of the scratches for the final game of the regular season, when John MacLean scored the game-winner in a 4–3 victory over Chicago.

But Shanny ran out onto the ice in his suit and dress shoes. So did the other scratches.

"We were all young," Shanahan said. "I was nineteen. [Sean] Burke was twenty-one. Our go-to guys were just twenty-three."

It was an incredible stretch for the Devils. Unbeaten over the final eight games of that regular season, New Jersey was headed for its first playoff appearance, taking a kid who ran all over the ice while wearing his good suit with them.

THE NEXT-BEST FEELING

Kenny, Kirk, and Beeker were all with the team when they finally made the playoffs during the 1987–88 season.

"We were seeing ourselves turning the corner," Daneyko said. "All the lean years were worth it. It's a little more gratifying when you grew up with the organization."

They made the playoffs on the final day of the season, a day Kenny calls "the next best feeling to winning the Cup."

FIRST PLAYOFF GOAL

Craig Wolanin was not the guy you'd expect to score the first playoff goal in team history. A stay-at-home defenseman who had just 16 goals over five seasons with the Devils, Craig can remember just about every goal he ever scored.

"When you score forty over thirteen years," he said, "you remember them all."

It was during the first playoff series in 1988—Devils versus the New York Islanders—that Wolanin got that first goal for New Jersey.

"The puck kind of squirted off the high point," Wolanin said. "I wish I could tell you I was aiming top shelf."

He wasn't. He was just launching it at Isles goalie Billy Smith.

"When you get the puck [toward] the net," Wolanin said, "good things sometimes happen."

FIRST TIME'S THE CHARM?

Not content to let Johnny Mac's goal serve as a moment that would carry them through an entire off-season, the Devils went into the playoffs with an attitude.

And why not? They had closed out the regular season with 10 wins in 13 games.

"Timing is everything," Muller said. "We were on such a roll."

They drew the Islanders in Round 1. For a long time, the Islanders were the cream of the New York metropolitan hockey market. They won Cups. They had stars. And when the Devils entered the league, the Islanders beat them fourteen straight times.

This time was different.

"We weren't cocky," Muller said. "We were hungry, excited, a real tough team to play against. We walked in and beat a pretty good team in the Islanders."

Pat LaFontaine scored an overtime winner to give the Isles a 1–0 series lead. But after Game 1, it was all Devils. New Jersey won four of the next five to move into Round 2, capturing the team's first playoff series in the process.

"It was all new to us," Muller said. "We were just a young group of guys. We said, 'We worked hard to get here, let's just go for it.' We were pumped. We were hungry. I don't know if we ever sat back and said, 'What are our chances?'"

Their chances were good. They beat the Islanders in six, then the Washington Capitals in seven before bowing out to the Boston Bruins in the Wales Conference Finals after seven tough games.

THE SCHOENFELD INCIDENT

It happened after the game, in a corridor down by the Devils locker room. The Bruins had just beaten the Devils 6–1 in Game 3 of the Wales Conference Finals, and New Jersey coach Jim Schoenfeld was livid.

Jimmy got into an argument with Don Koharski, one of the on-ice officials who was working the game. "Eat another doughnut, you fat pig!" is the line everyone seems to remember, the line Jimmy screamed at Koho. What had officials more upset were allegations that Jimmy shoved Koho, a big-time no-no.

"I asked him, 'Did you hit him?' in a very closed-door conversation," said Devils general manager Lou Lamoriello. "He said he did not."

Lou backed his guy. He reasoned that the Devils were too young and too fragile a franchise to let the league impose an unfair suspension on them. He thought his organization needed to take a stand.

"I went to Dr. McMullen and told him I thought this could be one of the most significant decisions in franchise history," Lamoriello said. "We had to take action because we didn't get the respect. If we accept that, it's no different than accepting losses."

Jimmy coached Game 4 after the Devils got an injunction to prevent a suspension. New Jersey won that night, a 3–1 Devils victory that evened the series at 2–2. But Jimmy was suspended for Game 5. Rather than hand the coaching reins to one of Jimmy's assistants, Lou decided to take the reins himself.

"The major reason I went and no one else went was that I thought Jimmy had done such a great job," Lamoriello said. "I really didn't want anybody to go behind the bench and make any changes . . . I really thought we could win. I wanted to keep the continuity. Hopefully we could pull the game out and Jimmy would just get back there."

Lou got tagged with the loss in the first playoff game he ever spent behind the Devils bench. But Jim made it back and coached later in the series.

On Mother's Day, the day of Game 4 of the 1988 Wales Conference Finals between the Devils and Boston Bruins, Paul McInnis was in his usual spot, eating dinner in the off-ice officials' room, when John McCauley walked in, a panicked expression on his face. The referees were refusing to take part in the night's game because of the Don Koharski-Jim Schoenfeld altercation, where Schoenfeld had called Koharski a fat pig.

McCauley needed replacements. "Saturday and all day Sunday, the referees insisted that Schoenfeld be suspended," McInnis said. "And there was no one around from the league."

"[McCauley] walked in and told [supervisor of off-ice officials] Dick [Trimble], 'These guys have got to referee tonight,'" McInnis said.

McInnis and Vin Godleski, two of New Jersey's off-ice officials, got pressed into service, along with New York Islanders office official Jimmy Sullivan.

"We didn't have anything," McInnis said. "I wore a pair of Aaron Broten's skates. We had Devils sweatpants on. And I was the referee, so I wore Vinny's stripes. Those two guys just had the yellow warm-up shirts for the first period."

It was an odd night, but it got easier for McInnis, Godleski, and Sullivan as the game progressed.

"The first penalty was an easy one for me to call," McInnis said. "Sean Burke fired the puck over the glass.

"The second period, three or four fights broke out at one time. We handled that, got through that, and got the game in."

The Devils won 3–1, squaring the series at 2–2 as the series moved back up to Boston.

The following morning, McInnis showed up at the hockey rink he'd been managing in Yonkers. He was stuck at the Meadowlands until 2 a.m. the night before, and now here were all these television crews waiting for him at his home rink.

"Fortunately, everyone was good about it," McInnis said. "The players and coaches were very understanding."

FIRST PLAYOFFS

So many of the older guys love reminiscing over that push to the playoffs during the 1987–88 season. Sean Burke remembers the playoffs themselves, and how a young team came within a hair of playing for the Stanley Cup.

"Obviously it was a great little run to make the playoffs," Burke said. "But to knock off the Islanders and then beat Washington and take Boston to seven games was more than anybody expected."

Nerves? Not at that age. Burkey was still only twenty-one, and many of his teammates weren't much older.

"At that age," Burke said, "you think maybe every year's going to be like this."

In the years that followed, he learned few years would be like that one. But he made sure to enjoy each game that post-season.

"You kind of didn't really think about it," Burke said. 'You just came to the rink every day, went 100 percent, then moved on to the next one."

FIRST PAIN

On the other end of the dressing room, Ken Daneyko was upset. Kirk Muller peered over and realized the same emotions that were punching him in the gut had already taken some swings at Kenny.

Kenny and Kirk helped tug New Jersey seven games deep into the conference finals. But during that seventh game against Boston, the rope snapped. Reality hit.

"We almost put ourselves on the map," Muller said. "There was still that sense of disappointment when you know you're one game away."

It was 6–2 Boston, end of the run. Don't let the door hit you. "They ended up getting a big clutch goal that put them up two," Muller said. "That was pretty much the nail in the coffin."

All that winning, that miraculous run to within one game of the Cup, didn't make the pain any easier.

"You don't know when you're going to get this opportunity again," Muller said. "It took a few years for any of us to get back there. We were on such a fun run we didn't want it to end."

TURNING POINT?

So why was it so tough after 1988? Why did it take the Devils six more years before they caught another glimpse of the conference finals?

Blame the Pittsburgh Penguins.

When Lou Lamoriello looks back on those first-round playoff exits, he remembers Mario Lemieux and his two-time Stanley Cup champion Penguins as the main reason why New Jersey's players watched most of the playoffs at home on television.

"If we would have had more experience with winning, and if more people were used to what you have to go through to get there . . ." Lamoriello said, then maybe that first Stanley Cup might have arrived at the Meadowlands a little sooner than 1995. Twice during the early 1990s—once in 1991, again in 1993—the Pittsburgh Penguins busted the Devils' Stanley Cup hopes during a playoff series.

That first loss was a killer. In 1991, New Jersey and Pittsburgh went at each other's throats for seven games during the first round. The Devils held a 3–2 series lead, but Pittsburgh won Game 6 4–3 and Game 7 4–0 to vanquish New Jersey.

Later that postseason, Lemieux was carting the Stanley Cup around the ice.

In 1993, Pittsburgh needed just five games to bump the Devils from the playoffs. The Penguins were coming off back-to-back titles, a tough out for any team who crossed their path.

"They were great from that standpoint," said Chris Terreri, New Jersey's starting goalie for 11 of those 12 playoff games against the Penguins. 'You could see we were getting better every year. We pushed a couple teams to Game 7, but couldn't seem to get over the hump."

Chris remembers officials calling back one goal during Game 6 of that 1991 Patrick Division semifinal series, a costly decision in a game where New Jersey had a chance to knock out the Penguins.

"There was nothing we could do," Terreri said. "We never regained the lead. That's the way it goes. You just have to bounce back, try to put yourself in the situation [again]."

8

"HE CAN'T EVEN SKATE"

ONE THING ABOUT LOU LAMORIELLO: He can be very loyal. Ask Jan Ludvig. Jan was the first guy Lou traded after he became the Devils general manager in 1987.

"Every time I get a chance," Ludvig said, "I remind him of that."

But after Jan's career ended, Lou brought Jan back as a scout. He worked with David Conte and Marshall Johnston, cutting his teeth on the scouting end of the business.

One night he was in Montreal, eyeing up a visiting defenseman and trying to decide if he'd be a good fit for New Jersey. Seated next to Jan was Carol Vadnais, a guy who played 17 seasons in the National Hockey League and was now scouting for the Montreal Canadiens.

Jan was still green then, not sure exactly how to judge a player when you weren't on the ice with him. So he leaned over and tapped Vadnais on the arm.

"Vad," Ludvig said. "How about this guy here? You think he's any good?"

Vadnais reportedly said, "Are you kidding? Look at him. He can't even skate."

Ludvig was stunned. "I guess I know nothing," he told Vadnais. "I kind of liked the guy."

"He's just brutal," Vadnais said. "I wouldn't touch him with a fifteen-foot pole."

Jan went back to his hotel room for the night. The next day, he woke up and picked up the *Montreal Gazette*. The Canadiens wound up trading for the guy he'd been watching the night before.

Wait a minute. Would Vadnais really have lied to him? Jan came at Vadnais with a smile the next time they ran into each other.

"I said, I thought we were friends,'" Ludvig said. "He said, 'Rookie, live and learn. Welcome to North America.'"

BIG BIRD

Bob Sauve and Sean Burke were roommates during the late eighties. Bob was the veteran goalie, the one who spent many an afternoon offering pointers to his young counterpart.

"He was the consummate professional," Burke said. "He really showed me how to handle myself on and off the ice as a professional."

Bob also razzed him when he could. Bob had a smallish build, while Burkey measured 6-foot-4. One day, out of the blue, Bob told Burkey, "Geez, you're a Big Bird."

Big Bird: just like the character on *Sesame Street*. Bob spent a lot of time trying to get that nickname to stick.

"People started throwing some Big Birds on the ice," Burke said. "He'd grab them sometimes and have them over by the bench. He'd have his skate lace around their necks and would be dangling them over the sides of the boards during games. I'd look over and he'd have one of these Big Birds dangling by the neck."

After his career ended, Bob became an agent for hockey players. His son spent time with the Colorado Avalanche.

But whenever he sees Burkey, he still calls him Big Bird.

SAWED-OFF STICKS

Jim Korn and Pat Verbeek were always trying to outdo each other when they were playing for the Devils in the late eighties.

One practice, Beeker found Korn's shoes and nailed them to a bench. When Korn got back to the locker room, he tugged and tugged before realizing someone had attached them to the bench.

Beeker got a good laugh out of that one, until Korn threatened one of the team's equipment guys to find out who pulled the prank.

A few practices later, Beeker came out to the ice with three sticks. He put two on the bench, then went out to practice with the third. Korn was the one chuckling when Beeker took his first slapshot that morning; the wooden stick snapped right in half.

Beeker didn't think anything of it. He skated back to the bench, grabbed one of his spares, and then—crack!

Beeker eventually had to go back to the locker room and nose around for a few extra sticks. A few more snapped before he realized what had happened. Korn had sawed his buddy's sticks in half.

"He got me back," Verbeek said.

I'm pretty sure Korn never found his shoes nailed to the bench after that.

THE FIRST WAVE OF RUSSIANS

Of all his accomplishments in New Jersey, John McMullen used to beam most proudly over his efforts to bring Russian players into the NHL. It sounds unthinkable now—the idea that there weren't any Russians in the NHL—but back then, it wasn't.

"I can remember one of the owners saying, 'I'll be damned if I'll have a commie on my team'" McMullen said. "Today he must have seven [Russians]. We really changed the whole character of the game."

New Jersey wanted Slava Fetisov, drafting him in the eighth round of the 1983 NHL Entry Draft. He did not play a game in a Devils sweater until 1989. At one point, John actually went down to Washington, D.C. and met with an ambassador, trying to persuade him that Slava would be a great fit with the Devils.

"He said, 'You can't expect me to go back and suggest I'm going to take one of the best hockey players out of their group and let him come to New Jersey,'" McMullen said. "'And not only that, but let him play for a team called the Devils.'"

John battled with immigration officials. He battled with government officials. Finally, in 1989, the Devils introduced both Slava and Sergei Starikov as Devils at a press conference.

"Everybody was against it and understandably so," McMullen said. "But can you imagine a hockey league today without a Russian?"

Canadiens forward Alexander Perezhogin (42) chases New Jersey caption Patrik Elias (26) during the third period of a 5-2 Devils win. *Jeff Zelevansky/Icon SMI*

OH, THEY'RE OUR RIVALS!

Nobody told Sergei Starikov about the Devils-Rangers rivalry when he first arrived in New Jersey. He learned first-hand, when his team's initial exhibition game that season came against the Blueshirts.

"At the start of the second," Starikov said, "everyone started to fight."

Starikov was an original, a pioneer in the hockey world. On June 26, 1989, the Devils announced the signing of Starikov and Slava Fetisov. On July 7, the Devils held a press conference introducing the pair.

"We were the first two guys in all sports to come [from the Soviet Union]," Starikov said. "People did not believe that [was happening]. But in the Soviet Union, there was a change of life, change of style, a couple of revolutions."

The two had played for the Red Army team in Moscow, on a squad that beat the Devils 5–0 during an exhibition game at the Meadowlands. After moving here, there was a period of learning a new style of hockey.

Over there, passing and creativity were staples. Over here, firing the puck at the net and then rushing in after it was more common.

They learned. Soon players from Poland, Russia, and other European nations were making the trek over. Guys like Starikov and Fetisov grew to understand the feuds between teams like the Rangers and Devils.

"I knew it was a competition, but not [that it was] like war," Starikov joked.

NEVER SETTLED

It took Chris Terreri a long time to finally feel like he belonged in New Jersey. Coming out of Providence College, the native New Englander remembers his first few seasons as something like a whirlwind.

"I knew I had a chance to make the team right off the hop," Terreri said. "I hung there for half the year, didn't play the whole year."

Chris made seven appearances during the 1986–87 campaign and never did get a win. He spent time in Maine with the Mariners. He logged minutes in Utica. He was a member of the 1988 United States Olympic team.

Chris always had a suitcase ready, rarely sure which city he'd be heading to, which team he'd be playing for next.

"The first year I lived in a hotel the whole year," Terreri said. "That was the hardest thing. I never really felt settled."

Only after that Olympic year did Chris feel more secure as a goalie. Call it confidence. Call it experience. But once he played for a gold medal on those large sheets of Olympic ice, he no longer doubted whether he deserved a spot on an NHL roster.

"It was different then," Terreri said. "I don't want to say easier, but it was. I felt much more in control."

Tom McVie was a big help. He was in New Jersey's minor-league system then, teaching Chris stick-handling, off-ice strength work, and mental toughness.

"He treated you hard," Terreri said, "but yet he built your confidence. I owe a lot to him for getting me there."

All goalies need a break, and Chris finally got his at the opening of the 1989–90 hockey season. Sean Burke, a playoff hero from New Jersey's run to the Wales Conference Finals, was hurt at the start of that season. Chris got the nod opening night against Philadelphia. Guarding the pipes in Burkey's absence, Chris allowed just two goals in a 6–2 road victory over the Flyers.

After 11 appearances to start his career without a win, Chris finally had one. Plus, now he had some confidence.

"When you get to play," Terreri said, "things happen where you win some games. The things you're working on in practice, the things you've worked on in the minors, start to pay off."

FROM RUSSIA, WITH LOVE

It may not seem like that big a deal, but when some of the Devils picked up Alexei Kasatonov on the way to a restaurant, he was genuinely touched. Alexei was among the first wave of Russians to venture over to North America to try playing in the NHL.

He didn't know a word of English. Even the hockey was different.

"Coming from Russia," Kasatonov said after a Devils alumni game, "it was not just a different country, but a different system."

Alexei said he remembers Lou Lamoriello bringing in a special teacher to help him with both English and hockey. He remembers guys like Ken Daneyko, Bruce Driver, and Troy Crowder trying to lend a hand.

"Everyone just takes care of you and supports you," Kasatonov said. "Everywhere. On ice. Off ice."

Once he had settled in, Alexei had Lou asking him about other Russians, trying to pick his brain about guys like Valeri Zelepukin. Guys like Alexei paved the way for the Sergei Federovs and Pavel Bures and Alexei Kovalevs, all of whom became stars in the NHL.

1980 REUNION

Mark Johnson played for the United States team that won the gold medal in 1980. Slava Fetisov played for the Soviet

Union team that lost to Johnson and a group of college kids in the semifinals.

Two heated rivals. Two guys who wanted to beat each other at all costs back in 1980. Two guys who didn't really know each other until they met in New Jersey.

"You become friends and get to know a person in a different light," Johnson said. "As far as a barrier between countries, now we were friends. I really enjoyed getting to know them as people."

One of the first things Mark remembers about guys like Slava Fetisov, Alexei Kasatonov, and Sergei Starikov arriving in New Jersey was the cultural divide they had to overcome. When the first wave of Russians came over to the United States, many of them brought their wives. Johnson heard stories of how some of the wives would fill their shopping carts with steaks in the meat department.

"They would grab handfuls of it, thinking tomorrow it wouldn't be there," Johnson said. "Part of the education process for our teammates was, 'No, you can come back tomorrow. You don't have to take fifteen steaks. You can come back tomorrow and get another one.'"

English was another barrier. Mark and some of the other North American-born skaters went out of their way to teach English to the newcomers. To this day, Mark suspects they understood a lot more than they were willing to let on.

"It depends if they wanted to listen to you or not," Johnson said. "They played possum a lot of times. When they didn't want to understand or listen, they'd become confused really quickly."

Of all the guys who came over from Russia, Mark held the highest respect for Slava. After his playing career ended, Slava spent time as an assistant coach with New Jersey. In 2004, he was working as one of the highest-ranking sports officials back in Russia.

"You don't realize until you get to know him how big a star he was in his homeland, and how respected he was in his environment back in Moscow," Johnson said. "As we got to know him, we understood that respect expanded around North America."

9

ALWAYS WANTED TO STAY

AARON BROTEN WAS A BIG FAN of New Jersey. He had a place in Ridgewood where he lived for most of his eight seasons with the Devils.

"I didn't ever want to leave there," Broten said.

Then one day, his phone rang. Devils general manager Lou Lamoriello got Aaron on the phone early the morning of January 5, 1990. Lou sent him to the Minnesota North Stars for Bob Brooke, a guy who would play just 35 regular-season contests and five playoff games in a Devils sweater.

"I was caught off guard," Broten said. "I had no idea it was coming. It was a shock when I got the call in the morning."

A shock, because it was the first time Aaron had ever been traded. Aaron was one of the kids on that 1982–83 team that was actually still around when the team turned things around.

Two things "cushioned the blow," according to Aaron. He was getting the chance to play in Minnesota, the state where he was raised. And he was getting the chance to play with his brother, an opportunity he never got in New Jersey. In 2016, twenty-six years after he was traded, he was still on New Jersey's all-time Top-10 lists for points, goals, and assists.

THEY TRADED HIM? THEY TRADED ME?

Jim Korn and Craig Wolanin spent a lot of days riding to morning skates together. Their routine was no different on March 6, 1990, except there were trade rumors swirling around just about everyone in the Devils dressing room.

Craig had heard his name pop up in the days leading up to the NHL trade deadline. On the ride home after the morning skate, Craig asked Jim for advice.

"Know what?" Korn told him. "More than likely, if you're here after the morning skate, you're staying here."

So Craig went home. He went through his pregame rituals. Then he hopped in his car and left for the Meadowlands.

When he got there for the team's game against the St. Louis Blues, the locker stall across the room from him was empty.

"Where's Jim?" Wolanin asked.

"He got traded," he was told.

That didn't make Craig feel any better. At least the 3 p.m. deadline had passed; he could assume he was safe.

Ten minutes before seven o'clock, Devils coach John Cunniff approached Craig.

"Three minutes before we went out for warm-ups," Wolanin said, "Cunny came in and said, 'Craig, I need to see you in my office.'"

Craig, like Jim, had been traded. John explained to Craig that there had been a problem with the fax machines at the league office, so it took a little while for the paperwork to officially go through.

Martin Brodeur makes a save during the Devils' 7–6 shootout victory over the Toronto Maple Leafs on October 12, 2006. *AP Images*

Both passengers in that early morning car ride were leaving New Jersey.

"I remember going into the lounge area of the locker room, burying my head, and sobbing," Wolanin said. "Kirk Muller and Dano [Ken Daneyko] came up to me. Those were two of the first guys to console me. It was devastating, really devastating."

THE PICK OF A LIFETIME

What's tougher to believe: That nineteen players were taken before Martin Brodeur in the 1990 NHL Entry Draft, or that New Jersey, a team that had more than one quality goalie in its system, took Marty with Pick No. 20?

At the time, Sean Burke and Chris Terreri provided a nice 1–2 punch for the Devils. Chris was getting better every season. Burkey was the guy who led New Jersey to the Wales Conference Finals in 1988.

"We didn't really need a goalie," said David Conte, New Jersey's director of scouting.

Most experts were tabbing Trevor Kidd as the top goalie prospect that season. Conte and his cohorts in New Jersey's scouting department couldn't understand why. They liked Marty and eventually took him with the twentieth pick.

"In the draft we weren't looking for goalies," Conte said. "It's a good lesson. You better take the best players. We didn't have a guy like Marty Brodeur, and it's tough to get the jewelry."

Conte has three Stanley Cup championship rings, each one from a season when Marty was the starting net-minder for New Jersey.

MONREAL VERSUS NEW JERSEY

A walk through Montreal will take you by the Notre Dame Basilica, some inviting French restaurants, and streets that echo history.

Oh, and they like hockey in Montreal, too. They *really* like hockey. But not everybody who lives in Montreal is a Canadiens fan, just as not everyone who lives in the Bronx is a New York Yankees fan.

Players are celebrities there, much more so than they are in New Jersey. "Everybody knows who you are," said Claude Lemieux, a forward who played for both the Canadiens and the Devils.

Lemieux had two runs in New Jersey, his first beginning on September 4, 1990. On that day, Devils general manager

Lou Lamoriello sent Sylvain Turgeon north of the border and brought Lemieux aboard for the first time.

"It's definitely night and day," Lemieux said. "It was a big change. It pushed me to do more and more to become more competitive."

FIVE FOR FIGHTING

It began with a cheap shot—or at least Troy Crowder considered it a cheap shot. From his vantage point, all he saw was Detroit Red Wings forward Bob Probert taking his stick and giving New Jersey's Claude Lemieux an ugly whack to the side of the head.

"You don't do that to my teammate," Crowder said. "There happened to be a line change. I jumped over the boards and made a bee line for him."

Troy learned early in his career that fighting would be his meal ticket. In the first game he played in the Ontario Hockey League, Troy scored two goals in a period and a half. His coach immediately yanked him from the lineup.

"Why'd you bench me?" Crowder asked.

"You're not here to score goals," he was told.

Troy was a quick learner. He got to know penalty boxes rather well. So when he saw Bob strike Claude, he didn't hesitate.

Troy started the fight. He got in a few good punches. By the time the fight ended, Bob was bleeding. Troy had picked a fight with one of the best fighters in the game and left a winner.

Dave Maley, Troy's roommate on the road, started calling him "The King" and began asking, "How's The King doing?" just about every day. Troy remembers sitting down with the morning newspapers, surprised to find his name in boxing columns and wrestling columns.

"It was definitely the talk of the hockey world for quite a while," Crowder said.

The Devils would play the Red Wings twice that season. Hype stalked Troy and the Devils until he and Bob had their anticipated rematch that January.

"Everybody sensed I was little nervous," Crowder said. "The team was a little nervous."

Kirk Muller tried to break the tension. The night before the game, Kirk took it upon himself to nix the curfew. All the players went out, had a few drinks, and got back to the team hotel sometime around 1 a.m.

"We were a little tired," Crowder said. "A little hung over."

Nothing an afternoon nap couldn't cure. And it sure did loosen Troy up a little. He fought Bob twice that night. Bob started the first one.

"At the end of my shift, I was going back to the bench when he gave me a shove," Crowder said. "I should have just gone off. My ego, I guess. I'm not one to back down from a challenge."

Troy slipped during that fight and Bob was all over him.

Later that night, after another fight and five minutes in the penalty box, Devils coach John Cunniff told Troy, "The next time he's out there, I'm sending you after him."

Two games. Three fights. Doesn't seem like much, but it really made Troy's reputation as one of the top enforcers in the NHL.

SHANAHAN LEVELS

Brendan Shanahan left the Devils in 1991. Shanny likes saying his agent found "a loophole" in the free agent market. Most free agents were veterans, guys in their thirties. Shanny was twenty-two.

Twenty-two, but experienced. He'd already played four seasons in the league by then, suiting up for 281 games with New Jersey. In his final season in the Garden State, the 1990–91 campaign, Shanny scored 29 goals and put up 37 assists.

St. Louis wanted him, so they threw money his way. Plenty of money.

"I'm sure a lot of guys saw me sign in St. Louis and used me to say, 'I'm better than that guy.'" Shanahan said. "It was kind of the cusp of where the salaries started to change."

Lou Lamoriello, the Devils general manager, never had the chance to match. It was in Shanny's hands. The money was nice, but what Shanny really wanted was a chance to be *the guy*.

"It was putting pressure on myself to take the next step," he said. "I had fallen into a role in New Jersey I was happy with, but I wanted to go to another level." He found that in St. Louis, and then again in Detroit.

Does he have any regrets? It doesn't sound like it: "I don't ever question the decision I made," Shanahan said. "I won three Stanley Cups and played for an Original Six team."

MULLER'S EXIT

After seven seasons, not one of which he scored less than 17 goals or played fewer than 77 games, Kirk Muller was shown the door.

"Unfortunately, that year there was a contract problem," Muller said. "We couldn't get it done."

On September 20, 1991, Kirk was sent to Montreal as part of a four-player trade that brought Stephane Richer and Tom Chorske to New Jersey.

"It was tough," Muller said. "A lot of those guys were really family. Basically, we lived together, did everything together. It was a real family."

Kirk finished his Devils career with 185 goals and 335 assists. By the end of the 2003–04 season, only three players in team history had scored more goals than him while wearing a Devils jersey.

"In the long run," Muller said, "it worked out fine for everybody. I was able to go up to Montreal and win a Cup up there."

ARE WE STAYHNG THIS TIME?

Scott Stevens did not buy a house when he first arrived in New Jersey. He owned a home in the Washington, D.C. area, another in St. Louis, and an arbitrator ruled that he was headed to New Jersey as compensation for Brendan Shanahan's decision to sign with the Blues.

Imagine that: Scotty, one of the best defensemen the game has ever seen, playing for his third team in three seasons; Scotty, one of the most ferocious hitters the game has ever seen, was a little concerned about all this moving.

"We basically rented," Stevens said. "We were a little gun-shy."

Scott and his wife, Donna, were more gun-shy than you might think. According to Scott, they rented in New Jersey for four or five years before they were convinced this New Jersey thing seemed to be working out.

"I felt pretty good," Stevens said. "I thought the defense was pretty solid."

The Devils then had Slava Fetisov, Bruce Driver, and Alexei Kasatonov. Martin Brodeur was a few short seasons away from becoming the franchise goalie. A young defenseman named Scott Niedermayer was on his way to the top.

"A lot of good things happened," Stevens said.

You know how things turned out. Scotty stayed. The Devils won three Stanley Cups. Eventually, Scotty broke down and bought a house in New Jersey.

OUT FOR THE SEASON?

They are four words no hockey player ever wants to hear. When a doctor says "out for the season," you squirm. You curse. Sometimes you cry.

As the calendar flipped toward October back in 1991, those were the words John MacLean heard just before the regular season was set to start.

"I had come off three 40-goal seasons prior to that," MacLean said. "I was scoring more and more. I felt I was in the best shape [I'd ever been in], ready to go."

In 1990–91, the previous winter, Johnny Mac scored a career-best 45 goals, including 19 on the power play. He was

New Jersey's John MacLean, one of the top forwards in franchise history, fires a slapshot against Tampa Bay during the 2000 season. *Jim Leary/Getty Images*

on a line with Peter Stastny, a left-handed passer who worked well next to Johnny, a right-handed shooter.

Then in the final exhibition game before the 1991–92 season, Johnny Mac's chance to chase a fourth consecutive 40-goal campaign vanished.

"There was a scrum around the net," MacLean said. "Back then, everybody [was grabbing] everybody. I grabbed Brad Dalgarno of the Islanders. Somebody bumped us. I fell awkwardly and blew my knee out."

Johnny Mac scored 347 goals for the Devils, second-most in franchise history behind Patrik Elias's 408. He came back and had four 20-goal seasons after returning from his knee injury.

But as he got older, and as the team's style turned from offensive-oriented to defensive-minded, he never hit 40 goals again.

10

A KID AND TWO LEGENDS

IF ANY PICTURE IS TRULY WORTH a thousand words, it's the one
Scott Niedermayer has at home.

Niedermayer, one of the most graceful skaters to ever wear a
Devils sweater, remembers his first heart-pumping moment as
an eighteen-year-old with New Jersey.

The Devils were playing an exhibition game up in Providence
against the Boston Bruins. He was sitting on the bench, waiting for his chance, when New Jersey coach Tom McVie sent
him out onto the ice.

When Scotty made his NHL debut that season, he was
young. At eighteen years, one month, and fifteen days old,
he was the youngest player to ever hit the ice for New Jersey.
The emotions got to him now and then. That first time
McVie called his name, Scotty raced out and hit the first guy
he could.

"Not really my game," Niedermayer said. "But I was so
excited to be out there, and that's what happened."

The photo he has at home is a snapshot of his first official game with New Jersey, a night when his Devils were playing the rival New York Rangers. In the photo, Scotty is carrying the puck behind the net. New York Rangers forward Mark Messier is chasing him. And Scott Stevens is right behind Messier.

It's a picture of two legends and a kid who grew up in British Columbia.

"I got an assist," Niedermayer said. "I don't think we won though."

Years later, after winning the Stanley Cup, Niedermayer would get another great photo. Every player gets to keep the Cup for a day after winning it. On Niedermayer's day, he and the Cup made it to the very top of a mountain, where a picture was snapped of him holding it over his head. It's one of the most creative Cup photos I've ever seen.

HOLDING OUT

Sean Burke realized long after the fact that maybe a contract dispute wasn't the healthiest thing for his NHL career. He wound up sitting out the entire 1991–92 season before the Devils finally packaged him with Eric Weinrich in a trade with the Hartford Whalers.

"I was a little disappointed with the way I left," Burke said. "But I look back and realize I didn't handle things the way I would have handled it five years later."

The year wasn't a total loss. He played for the Canadian Olympic team in 1992 and went home with a silver medal. He got in a few games with the San Diego Gulls of the International Hockey League while he was holding out.

"There wasn't bitterness," Burke said. "It was one of the best things that happened to me. I wound up going back, playing for the Olympic team. I came back here and had even more of an appreciation for the opportunity to be able to play in this league."

The trend continued; by the end of his career, Burkey had played for eight different NHL franchises.

LOUISVILLE SKATE

It was just an exhibition game, but Tom McVie was fuming. Upset with the way his players treated a preseason game against the Hartford Whalers in Louisville, Kentucky, he woke up the boys early the following morning and had them running through drills.

"He had us skating for an hour and a half with no pucks," said New Jersey forward Claude Lemieux. "Every time I skated up ice, I thought it had to be the last time."

To make matters worse, some of the players had been out really late the previous night, so the early wake-up call was a killer.

When the skating finally ended, Claude wanted nothing to do with his coach.

"I didn't want to talk to him, didn't want to see him," Lemieux said.

Most of the players were sitting at the airport, slumped over with exhaustion in their seats, when Tom showed up for the flight. He must have known he needed something to diffuse the tension.

"He came running down the terminal and dropped his bag," Lemieux said. "In his suit and raincoat, he started walking on his hands. He was [about] sixty years old. We all cracked up. You couldn't help but love the guy."

I TRIED TO CALL YOU!

They snapped a team picture of the 1991–92 Devils on one of the first few days after Martin Brodeur got called up for the first time. Chris Terreri and Craig Billington, New Jersey's top two goalies at the time, were battling injuries. The Devils brought up two kids from the minors and Brodeur from the Quebec Major Junior Hockey League. It was kind of rare to see; it isn't often you see a team carrying five goalies.

When they lined up for the photo, Marty was told to wait off the ice—sorry kid, no more room.

According to Marty, the other four guys, even the minor league guys, made the picture.

"These guys were in the minors the whole year," Brodeur said. "They figured they'd put them in there."

He actually watched the first game after his call-up from the stands at the Meadowlands. Even with the injuries, Marty wasn't the backup.

The morning of his second game up with the team, Devils coach Tom McVie threw a good scare into his nineteen-year-old net-minder.

"Where were you last night?" McVie screamed at Brodeur. "I tried to call you!"

"Now I was like, 'Oh my God! Did I sleep through a phone call?'" Brodeur said. "I was so nervous."

McVie gestured away from the ice, telling Marty, "Come with me up to my office."

"Oh no," Brodeur said he remembers thinking. "Here we go."

But McVie was pulling a prank on his young goalie. He wasn't calling Marty in for a tongue-lashing; he was calling him in to let him know he'd be starting that night.

"Robbie Ftorek was the assistant coach," Brodeur said. "He grabbed me and said, 'You get on the phone right now and call your parents and your friends. Tell them to come down. It's going to be a fun day.'"

The relatives made it down from Montreal in time to watch Marty carry a shutout deep into the third period. He wound up with the first win of his career, a 4–2 victory over the Boston Bruins.

Marty won 691 games during his NHL career. The run of wins began that March night in 1992, after McVie pulled a fast one on him.

CULTURE SHOCK

Culture shock is going from Jihlava, Czech Republic, to Hartford, Connecticut. Jihlava is the city where Bobby Holik was born. Hartford is the city where Bobby first got his start in the National Hockey League.

Then Bobby switched again. He was traded from Hartford, a relatively small market, to New Jersey, a market that attracts the New York City dailies.

"Coming to New Jersey was a great thing," Holik said. "It was a time when the organization was finding its own identity."

Bobby's arrival coincided with the departure of goalie Sean Burke. On August 28, 1992, Burkey went north and Bobby came south, I've seen a lot of Bobby over the years, and he reminds me of Bryan Trottier, a guy I used to play with on the Islanders.

A few seasons after he arrived in New Jersey, Bobby was playing between Randy McKay and Mike Peluso on the unforgettable Crash Line.

"[Coach Jacques Lemaire] just had a vision of what he want-ed the team to be," Holik said. 'You kind of accepted the role you were given and made the most of it."

Jacques was good for Bobby. Then again, Jacques was good for a lot of the guys on those early nineties Devils teams.

"He was one of the greatest influences on me in profession-al hockey," Holik said. "When I turned pro and came to the NHL, he made the difference. He showed us how to win, how to play winning hockey."

Winning made the culture shock disappear in a hurry.

HE KEPT CALLING ME AND CALLING ME . . .

Jacques Lemaire had been a winner long before he ever stood behind benches and podiums in New Jersey. Jacques scored the game-winning goal for the Montreal Canadiens in the fourth and deciding game of the 1977 Stanley Cup Finals, then again had the series-clinching goal in 1979.

And that's exactly what New Jersey general manager Lou Lamoriello loved about Jacques.

"Somebody had to walk into the room who had the expe-rience of winning," Lamoriello said. "His presence was signif-icant."

Lou began placing calls to Montreal general manager Serge Savard, asking for permission to interview Jacques. At the time, Jacques was the Canadiens' assistant general manager.

"I never thought about coaching," Lemaire said. "I never thought about going back and coaching a team."

Three or four times, Serge told Jacques that Lou was inter-ested. Three or four times, Jacques didn't bother returning Lou's call.

"One day [Serge] came in and said, 'Why don't you call him?'" Lemaire said. "I did call him, and then he said he wanted to meet."

Lou brought Jacques in for an interview in 1993, not long after he'd handed Herb Brooks his walking papers. Lou didn't beat around the bush.

"I feel we can win the Cup," Lamoriello told Lemaire. "There's a missing link, and it's something that has nothing to do with the [team's] physical capabilities, and you can bring that."

Jacques accepted the job, even though Lou had fired five different head coaches in his six seasons as general manager.

"I flew there and looked at it, and I just felt that it would be a great place," Lemaire said.

Within two seasons, Jacques brought Lou exactly what he wanted.

THE INNOVATOR

I never thought of Jacques Lemaire as a defensive forward. During his 853-game playing career, Jacques scored 366 goals and had 469 assists, averaging just under a point a game.

He played on a line with Steve Shutt and Guy Lafleur in Montreal. Every guy on that line was a threat to score.

So it was funny that when Jacques arrived in New Jersey, he installed a trap-heavy system many teams have since mimicked.

"I think it was part of my game all the time, part of my thinking all the time, even as a player," Lemaire said. "I was telling Lafleur to stay up, stay on offense all the time, I'll take care of the backchecking. I was telling Shutt, 'Make sure you cover me when I'm up.'"

Lou Lamoriello wore many hats for the Devils. In 2006, he was behind the bench during New Jersey's playoff series against the Carolina Hurricanes. Carolina would win that series in five games. *AP Images*

Clogging up the middle was just one of his innovations. Another was his heavy use of a checking line. Randy McKay, Mike Peluso, and Bobby Holik became known as the Crash Line. Rarely before had a coach given a checking line twelve to fourteen minutes a game.

"When there's something new, people worry," Lemaire said. "It takes a while. Look at when [Wayne] Gretzky came in. The way he was playing was new. Everyone was scared."

According to Jacques, Bobby actually asked to be moved off the line during the season. Jacques said Bobby wanted to play on a line that contributed more offensively.

"I told him, 'You've got pretty much the best line on our club right now. Why do you want to change?'" Lemaire said. "They were a line that changed the game a lot. I could put them out at any time."

Jacques made Bobby a better player. He had a big smile on his face the day his former pupil signed a $45 million contract with the New York Rangers.

I just hope Bobby remembered to send Jacques a thank-you note.

THE GREAT JACQUES

Jacques Lemaire still has the panoramic photo of that first Cup hanging on a wall at home. He won the Stanley Cup for the first time as a coach with the Devils in 1995, but really won the team over when he came aboard for the start of the 1993–94 season.

"He got instant respect from everybody," said New Jersey forward Claude Lemieux. "There were no two ways. There was one way: his way. He's a brilliant guy."

It sounds funny coming from Claude. His strength was scoring, yet his offensive numbers plummeted in New Jersey after Jacques took the reins. After scoring 30 goals in three straight seasons, Claude put up just 18 during the first season of the Jacques Lemaire Era.

"I knew I was going to have a drop in production just because of the style he was going to have us play," Lemieux said.

The concept was simple. Defense, defense, defense. Trap, trap, trap.

"The system was built for the team that we had," Lemieux said. "He got everybody to believe in it. He wasn't one of those guys who made you skate so hard. He just made everything very clear how to get it done, [emphasizing] penalty killing and rolling four lines of most of time."

CAR ACCIDENT

Jacques Caron was in the passenger's seat, squinting, the glare of the sun making it impossible for either him or his buddy to get a clear view out of the car's front window. It was 7:30 a.m. They were driving up a hill, on their way to a Hartford Whalers practice, when another car smashed into them.

Jacques survived the wreck, but his hip took a beating. Until the accident, he had been the Whalers' goalie coach. After the accident, he figured maybe it was time to call it a career.

"I didn't even think about coming back," Caron said. "I never thought I'd be into hockey again."

He had an apartment in Binghamton. When his hip was cooperating, he'd head over and watch the local minor league team play.

It was there that he first saw Martin Brodeur, the goalie who brought him back into the National Hockey League, the goalie he would tutor for the next decade.

"I didn't even know he existed until I saw him play in Binghamton," Caron said. "He got beaten 7–4, but I liked his ability and his size."

It was enough of a carrot to entice Jacques to return to professional hockey when the Devils put in a call to his apartment, asking if he would be interested in joining the team as a goaltending coach.

DAWN OF AN ERA

Lou Gehrig, the Iron Horse, the guy who once played 2,130 straight baseball games with the New York Yankees, only got his start when Wally Pipp sat out a day with a headache. Few can appreciate that tidbit of trivia the way Martin Brodeur can.

After making his National Hockey League debut in 1992, Marty thought he'd get a shot to play the following season.

He didn't.

"I didn't play a preseason game," Brodeur said. "They sent me right to the minors."

He spent 32 games in Utica during the 1992–93 season. He didn't make a single appearance with the Devils.

That summer, backup goalie Craig Billington was shipped to Ottawa as part of a trade that brought Peter Sidorkiewicz to Jersey. Sidorkiewicz had shoulder problems that autumn, opening the door for Marty.

"[If] he comes in healthy," Brodeur said, "maybe I'm not going to play in the NHL that year."

But Marty split time with Chris Terreri that season. Even when Sidorkiewicz came back, Jacques Lemaire stayed with Marty.

'You could see he had poise above his years," said Randy McKay, one of Brodeur's first teammates.

They had faith in him, even back then. When the Rangers finally ended New Jersey's dream season in May of 1994, Marty had started 17 of New Jersey's 20 playoff games, including all seven in the big series against New York.

11

THE CRASH LINE

RANDY MCKAY DIDNT TAKE TOO MANY BEATINGS when he was with the Devils. One of the few losses he remembers came against Florida, when Paul Laus punched out three of his teeth.

No loss, no matter how many of his teeth it involved, stopped Randy from dropping the gloves and going after someone else.

"One year," McKay said, "we [McKay and teammate Mike Peluso] both had 28 majors."

In McKay and Peluso, Devils coach Jacques Lemaire saw something he could exploit. The year before the Devils won their first Stanley Cup, Lemaire put the duo on a line with a young centerman named Bobby Holik. The trio formed the unforgettable Crash line, a line that could go from beating up some poor opponent one moment to injecting offensive momentum the next. They became fan favorites at the Meadowlands.

"Mike and I both knew our roles," McKay said. "We were the enforcers. A lot of nights we both had one or two fights each. But we were pretty smart about it."

McKay averaged 232 penalty minutes a season during his first three campaigns with New Jersey. Peluso logged 236 penalty minutes the first year Lemaire put the trio together.

What impressed McKay most was what he noticed several years later, after the three members of the line had gone their separate ways. Around the NHL, he saw other teams mimicking what the Devils had done.

"As far as size goes and production goes," McKay said, "we were a model for what teams tried to copy and do."

PUGILISTS TO LINEMATES

Mike Peluso and Randy McKay used to fight all the time, back when Mike was in Chicago and Randy was in Detroit. In Randy, Mike saw a player who mirrored many of the qualities he possessed.

For years, on days when their two teams weren't playing each other, Mike would pick up the paper and thumb through it until he found the box score from Randy's game. The respect was always there. Maybe that's what made it easy for them to not only co-exist, but to co-exist and thrive as linemates in New Jersey.

"I don't really think about the fights we had in the past because of what we went through as teammates," Peluso said.

The Crash Line was one of the most popular lines to ever come through the Meadowlands.

"There will never be another line like that," Peluso said. "We drew four to five penalties a game. We'd go out there and take the body, add a lot of energy to the building. We kind of woke up everybody. I was fortunate to play with those guys."

WINNING IS ATTITUDE

As many of the Devils will readily attest, Bobby Holik can be hard on his teammates. The beat writers loved Bobby. He was opinionated and exceedingly quotable, but the big thing with Bobby was that he never shied away from calling out the Devils when they weren't playing well as a team.

Bobby loves winning, even more so than most of the guys you'll find in NHL dressing rooms. He always had that attitude, but former New Jersey coach Jacques Lemaire fanned the flames of Bobby's animosity toward losing.

"The way he lived, the way he carried himself, it's attitude," Holik said. "Winning is attitude. Or winning is a culture of life. The way you come to practice, the way you take care of yourself, the way you travel, the way you carry yourself before games, the way you play games: that's winning."

Bobby learned to play hockey when he was just five. Then, same as now, Bobby wanted to win, or at the very least put himself on a path where winning was an attainable goal.

"Winning is overwhelming," Holik said. "It's very hard to express what it's like. . . . Do you have goals? Do you want to accomplish something? When you do, that's like winning the Stanley Cup. A lot of people don't reach those goals. The most fun part is trying your hardest to get it. Not everybody will get it. Life is not perfect. Life is not fair. I feel very fortunate I've won it twice."

MR. ENERGY

He had long hair. He was vocal. He tried to get the crowd involved as much as possible.

Fans sure did get a kick out of Mike Peluso during his four seasons in Jersey. When he played for Mike Keenan in

Chicago, Keenan demanded Mike come out with as much energy as possible. Mike made injecting energy into a dead team or a dead game his calling card.

"If there was no energy in the building," Peluso said, "I tried to provide it."

The first season he arrived in New Jersey, there was Keenan on the opposing bench, coaching the New York Rangers. After he left Chicago, playing against Keenan always sent Mike's emotions into overdrive.

He fought a lot too, endearing himself to the fans who made the trek to the Meadowlands. Even now, when fans ask about his hockey career, he begins by mentioning his career in New Jersey.

"I played a lot of places," Peluso said. "But I always say I played for the Devils."

IN YOUR FACE

Claude Lemieux was most certainly not Mr. Nice Guy. Away from the game, he got along with people just fine. But at the rink, look out.

"I was not the most pleasurable player to be around," Lemieux said. "To me, it has always been about winning. Guys who are just happy-go-lucky every day usually don't end up getting much done at work on the ice. You have to put in everything."

Devils general manager Lou Lamoriello liked Claude, probably for that very reason. Claude did two tours with New Jersey, alternately drawing praise for his work ethic and ire for the way he dealt with some of the other guys in the locker room.

"I think I was very demanding of myself and of my teammates," Lemieux said. "I was willing to do whatever it took to win."

Claude would say anything to anybody. One time he was bold enough to walk right up to New Jersey captain Scott Stevens and chew him out over something he didn't like.

"It got pretty heated," Lemieux said. "I think from that point on we talked more, got on the same page. It's good to have people with character, with their own ideas. You don't want a bunch of yes men, guys without pride or desire or personality."

Now that he's retired from the game, Claude understands his in-your-face style was not for everyone.

"I had a tough streak for a couple of years," Lemieux said. "I was going through my divorce. I didn't play very well. It must have been hard being around me."

Hard, sure. But when Claude was on the ice, more often than not his team won hockey games.

SHOOTING HIGH

Goalies hate it when teammates shoot high on them in practice. Take it from me—I've been there. Taking a puck to the head stings, facemask or no facemask.

Mike Peluso learned this the hard way. He went high in practice one day, probably took an earful from the goalie. He got what was coming to him the following day, when he was changing for practice.

"You're in a hurry to get out on the ice, to make the practice so you're not late," Peluso said. "The last things you put on are your skates. I get to my skates, and the laces are all cut."

It took Mike about ten minutes before he found replacement laces and had them on his skates. By then, he was late for practice.

Mike never did learn who put the scissors to his laces. But he has a guess.

GORDIE HOWE HAT TRICK

According to the 2003–04 Devils media guide, New Jersey players had recorded 57 hat tricks since the 1982–83 season. There's no official stat for "Gordie Howe hat tricks"—an odd stat termed for players who have scored a goal, earned an assist, and gotten into a fight all during the same game.

Mike Peluso remembers one he had against the Florida Panthers during his time with the Devils. He already had the assist. He'd fought twice. But it was a tight game, and Mike still needed a goal.

How fitting that Mike was the guy who scored the game-winner that night, completing his Gordie Howe hat trick.

"I went to the net, Bobby [Holik] threw it in front, and I tapped it in," Peluso said. "After I retired, I told everybody I went end to end like Paul Coffey."

TOUGH MINUS

Rangers fans love hearing "Matteau! Matteau!" They can't get enough of it. But that name makes Devils fans cringe.

Stephane Matteau ended a phenomenal back-and-forth series, the 1994 Eastern Conference Finals, with his legendary overtime goal in Game 7. It was Martin Brodeur's rookie season, New Jersey's first realistic shot at making it to the Stanley Cup Finals. Matteau and the New York Rangers crushed that dream during overtime of that seventh game.

Scott Niedermayer admits he has trouble remembering games that were played ten years back. But he remembers that one.

"I was on [the ice] for the winning goal against [us]," Niedermayer said.

CHAPTER 11

It was a tough game, a tough series, and a tough memory for Niedermayer, even though he said it was great to be involved in a series that has its own special place in NHL history. If it weren't for those three Stanley Cups he would win with New Jersey, Niedermayer might look back at that shift with more disdain.

"It's worth more than minus-one," Niedermayer said.

COSTLY MISTAKES

Even if they had played their absolute best, Bruce Driver still isn't sure whether his Devils would have won that 1994 Eastern Conference Finals series against the New York Rangers. But what still gnaws at Brucey are the mistakes his team made after taking a 3–2 series lead.

"We had them on the ropes," Driver said. "We made mistakes in that game that we hadn't made in months."

New Jersey was actually up 2–0 in Game 6, a few periods away from moving on to the franchise's first Stanley Cup Finals. Then Rangers forward Alexei Kovalev scored, cutting the lead to 2–1 and setting the stage for an unforgettable New York comeback.

"The goal we gave up at the end of the second period that changed the momentum of the game was a bad line change," Driver said. "And we didn't have bad line changes. That was something that was one of our traits. We got caught on a bad line change, and it turned into a 3-on-2, and they scored on it."

Even as the series slipped away, Brucey remembers New Jersey still being in it up until that final Stephane Matteau shot.

"If you go back and watch Game 7," Driver said, "[you'll see] we had a glorious chance fifteen seconds before they scored in overtime to win the series. Bernie Nicholls had a wide-open net. I don't know . . . a bounce, a hook, or whatever, but that's the game of hockey."

It was exhausting. And at the time, it hurt. Only years later was Brucey glad he was a part of that series. He thinks it helped the Devils prepare for their run in 1995.

"People still talk about that series," Driver said. "Especially on the East Coast. We hear so much about the seven-game series against the Rangers. A lot of people here who aren't Rangers fans don't even know who the Rangers played in the Stanley Cup Finals."

AM I EVER GOING TO WIN IT?

Of all the players crushed by that Game 7 loss to the New York Rangers, Scott Stevens may have taken it the hardest.

"It was hard to swallow, obviously," Stevens said. "It took thirteen years to win that first Cup. That was twelve years [of my career] without a Cup. It was tough."

A loss of that ilk made even a great player like Scotty wonder if maybe a Cup win wasn't in the cards. Maybe he was doomed to go an entire career without ever harvesting the dream he planted back in Kitchener, Ontario as a kid.

There's a long list of players who have come through the National Hockey League who have never gotten their paw prints on the Stanley Cup. Scotty wanted off that list, pronto.

"We knew we had some good years ahead of us," Stevens said. "We got back at it."

12

LOCKOUT? NOT NOW

MOST OF THE DEVILS WERE BURNING to get back out on the ice after losing that 1994 series to the Rangers.

A lockout made that next to impossible. Players waited and waited and waited for a new season to open, trying to squeeze in workouts whenever they could.

Bruce Driver had one of the toughest assignments. He was a player rep and an assistant captain. As player rep, he was keeping players up to speed on the status of the Collective Bargaining Agreement. As assistant captain, he was trying to gather as many teammates together as possible for practices at South Mountain Arena.

"It's not like we were doing wind sprints or high-level drills," Driver said. "We were just skating and scrimmaging. I just tried to take the mind-set that the more we kept guys together, kept guys skating, it might [give us] a slight edge. I don't know if it helped at all."

During the lockout, players weren't allowed to use team facilities. So Brucey and some of the other players chipped in to rent ice time. They steered clear of the main Devils dressing room, changing into their gear in the same tiny rooms the local high school and pee wee teams used. They invited a few local kids over to fill in open spots during scrimmages.

When the season finally did resume, the Devils were frothing at the mouth. By June, the Devils were Stanley Cup champions for the first time.

Brucey said he didn't know if those early sessions helped. I think they did.

FROM CHECKER TO SCORER

He came into the National Hockey League as a scoring threat, but after a while, Neal Broten found himself playing on checking lines. His coaches loved putting him out there against other teams' top lines, using him the way future Devils coaches would use Bobby Holik and John Madden.

On February 27, 1995, New Jersey general manager Lou Lamoriello sent Corey Millen to Dallas, bringing Neal to New Jersey. Neal's brother Aaron played 581 games in New Jersey, but it was Neal who would later score some of the biggest goals in team history.

Jacques Lemaire, the coach of that 1995 Devils team, decided against using Neal as a checker.

"Jacques recognized I had some ability to play," Broten said. "I played with John MacLean and Claude Lemieux. We produced. It was fun to be an offensive player again."

For years, Neal was lining up against guys like Detroit Red Wings forward Steve Yzerman and some of the NHL's other top forwards.

"You're not thinking offensively," Broten said. "So your production goes down."

But that Devils team had Bobby Holik, Mike Peluso, and Randy McKay playing together. Jacques saw no need to shackle the offensive talent he recognized in Neal Broten.

Neal was terrific down the stretch run for that '95 team, scoring eight goals and adding 20 assists over the team's final 30 contests. He averaged almost a point a game during his first season in a Devils sweater.

"We just played really good hockey," Broten said. "Our defense held. The gap between our forwards and defensemen was nice and tight. And Jacques was just a really intelligent coach. I loved the way he coached, the way he approached hockey, the way he treated his players."

(DEFENSE) MAN TO (DEFENSE) MAN

So many fans only know Scott Stevens as the wrecking ball who made a career of storming up and down the ice, throwing fear into opponents. For a while, that portrait wasn't entirely inaccurate.

"When I first got there," said former Devils head coach Larry Robinson, "his biggest fault was his temper. I think he's learned to control that the most. It's made him more of a complete player. He's a lot more in control of his emotions."

Larry was an assistant on the '95 team that won the Stanley Cup. The Hall of Fame defenseman's main responsibility was improving the defense, ensuring none of his blue-liners tried to do too little or too much.

Larry says he never tried to change the core of a player. A rock-'em, sock-'em forward was a rock-'em, sock-'em forward. A slick-skating defenseman was a slick-skating defenseman.

Scott Stevens was on the way to the Hall of Fame. But Larry saw a veteran player who could be even better if he could trim the time he spent in the penalty box.

"When I first came up," Robinson said, "I was a hot head, too. I would take a lot of dumb penalties, put my team at risk. [Realizing] that was the one thing that really, really helped me get control of my emotions."

The more Scotty aged, the fewer penalties he committed. Instead of putting up 120 or 150 penalty minutes a season, Scotty was down to 70 or 80. In 2002–03, the season when New Jersey won its third Stanley Cup, Stevens logged what was then a career-low 41 minutes in the penalty box.

"When I spoke to him," Robinson said, "I tried to relay some of my own personal experiences. If you've had success, it's a lot easier when you're talking to someone than if you've never won anything and you're trying to get a point across."

MARTY'S FIRST RING

Joe Louis Arena is no picnic. Not for veterans, not for kids. But that's where the Devils headed the first time they made the Stanley Cup Finals, opening a series in Detroit against the Red Wings.

Martin Brodeur, normally the calmest guy in the locker room, remembers being a little intimidated by both the Red Wings and the building.

"I didn't play there my first year," Brodeur said. "My second year, I had the lockout. It was the first time I was playing in Detroit. It's a pretty special place to play."

The Devils swept the series. Marty never allowed more than two goals in any game that series. So much for intimidation.

Jacques Lemaire, the first coach to bring the Stanley Cup home to New Jersey, announced his resignation on May 8, 1998. Many credit Lemaire for talking the franchise to new heights. *AP Images*

"It was so weird," Brodeur said. "We were so afraid of them. The next thing you know, we'd won the Stanley Cup."

Looking back, Marty said he thinks the novelty of playing in the Finals may have made his stomach a little less queasy.

"I didn't really see a lot of ups and downs compared to now, when you know what's ahead," Brodeur said. "When you've never won it, I think you just go through it [and think], 'Hopefully it's going to happen.' When your expectations are higher, you have a different way of dealing with adversity."

MR.GAME-WINNING GOALS

When Neal Broten got his chance to take a spin around the ice with the Stanley Cup above his head, he knew he'd done more than enough to help the Devils beat Detroit.

Neal was the guy who scored the game-winning goal in Game 3 of that Stanley Cup Finals series against the Detroit Red Wings. He was the guy who scored the game-winner in Game 4, the night when New Jersey first brought the Cup to the Garden State.

"We were pretty confident going in," Broten said. "Everyone else picked Detroit. I thought we had a pretty good team."

In Game 3, he scored twice in New Jersey's 5–2 win. "I think we had a pretty good lead," Broten said. "I scored a couple late goals. I didn't think [either one] was going to be the game-winning goal."

It put New Jersey up 3–0 in the series, one win from not only beating the Red Wings, but sweeping them.

In Game 4—another 5–2 Devils victory—Neal did it again.

"If I'm thinking right," Broten said, "it was a fluke. It went off a foot, hit my stick, and went in the net. It was not a real pretty goal. But going behind the goal line is all that counts."

What a night for Neal Broten. In 2007, he was one of only three guys on the planet who could brag about scoring a Stanley Cup Finals series-clinching goal while wearing a Devils uniform.

EMOTIONS POUR OUT

With five minutes to go in Game 4 of the 1995 Stanley Cup Finals, the Devils sitting on a 5–2 lead, Ken Daneyko looked down the bench and spotted Mike Peluso crying.

Mike Peluso: the guy who never met a penalty minute he didn't like, one of the wingers on the Crash Line.

"It was pretty emotional," Daneyko said. "I remember [Detroit coach] Scotty Bowman saying he was embarrassed [about the loss]," Daneyko said. "But [our win in Game 3] was more about how well our team had played and how we had come together as a team. By Game 4 we were on cloud nine. I'm surprised we were able to play so well and stay so evenly keeled."

THREE ORIGINALS

The Devils won three Stanley Cups over a nine-season stretch, but none offered the impact or the catharsis of that first one. It was a shock when Game 4 of that 1995 series rolled around, and the Devils were sitting on a 3–0 lead against the Red Wings.

"When we got back to our building [up 2–0]," said Bruce Driver, "we almost felt like we had them. We knew what we were doing. They had to make adjustments to us."

Randy McKay and Brucey both remember entering as heavy underdogs given little chance to win by the pundits.

"I'll never forget," McKay said. "Four of the five papers were picking us to lose four straight. The other one picked us to lose in three straight. They said we'd be so embarrassed after three, we wouldn't show up for four."

Show up they did. And when they won the Cup, the celebration erupted.

"I looked at John MacLean and Ken Daneyko," Driver said. "The three of us together since not Day One, but darn near Day One, during all those years of frustration, of not having good teams or not making the playoffs, and after the disappointment of the year before. We just looked at each other and said, 'We just won the Stanley Cup.'"

The Devils and Nets shared a training room at the time. Brucey, Kenny, and Johnny Mac tried sneaking through the training room into the Nets locker room. Brucey wanted a photo of the three of them together with the Cup, something away from the television cameras.

No such luck.

"A horde of media followed us," Driver said. "There were so many pictures taken. I've got my picture framed. I know there's a ton of others out there, but mine means a lot to me."

REPLAYING THE SERIES

A crossbar. A missed breakaway. A turnover.

John MacLean's mind raced through the highlights often that summer after the Rangers knocked out his Devils in seven games. He searched every game, trying to find some spot where he could have been better, where his team could have been better.

"A goal here, a goal there," MacLean said. "What if we'd scored there?"

He would replay the final few games of the final series of 1995 too, but those were replays of what went right: a Devils goal; a Martin Brodeur stop; a home crowd going absolutely berserk.

"Some guys win it their first year in the league," MacLean said. "They work just as hard, but sometimes they don't appreciate what went into it. This organization didn't always win every year. A 100-point season starts with 48-point seasons, when you're out of the playoffs."

THE ORCHESTRA

So what happened? How did a team go from winning the Stanley Cup one season (1994–95) to missing the playoffs entirely the following season (1995–96)?

"Very simple," said Devils general manager Lou Lamoriello. "We had almost won [one year, then] we won [the next]."

Lou also believed that the guys he always counted on as role players and support players began to envision themselves as something brighter.

"It's no different than in a car, when you give gas to your ignition," Lamoriello said. "If you don't have a strong carter pin, no matter how strong the pistons are and the engine is, there's a problem. What happened was our carter pins, in their minds, became pistons. And people who were getting eight minutes [a game] thought that they should be getting twelve and fourteen because all summer people had been telling them how good they were."

Around that time, Lou came up with his orchestra analogy. Not too many people would liken a hockey team to a symphony you'd see at the New Jersey Performing Arts Center, but that's what Lou did. He wanted his drummers to drum. He wanted his violinists to focus on playing the violin. In hockey terms, he didn't want a big defenseman like Ken

Daneyko taking the puck all the way up ice and trying to score goals.

"Kenny's a great example for the orchestra," Lamoriello said. "As I've always said to him, when he thinks he's a violinist, he's in trouble and we're in trouble. And he knows that. He understood it."

13

WRITING ON THE WALL

ON NOVEMBER 15, 1995, Chris Terreri was shipped out to San Jose for a second-round draft pick. He knew it was coming. By then, Martin Brodeur owned a Calder Trophy, the starting job, and had led the Devils to their first Stanley Cup title. Chris was caught at the intersection of Wrong Place and Wrong Time.

"They were going to move somebody," Terreri said. "I was the best commodity at the time. They weren't going to trade Marty. They wanted to bring a couple kids along. It was an opportunity for me to go out and still play and play a lot."

He went out to San Jose, then later spent parts of seasons with the Chicago Blackhawks and New York Islanders. Before retiring, he came back to New Jersey for three more seasons with the Devils.

"I was close enough in my relationship with Lou [Lamoriello]," Terreri said. "He called me into his office a few days before it went down. We talked about it. I thought it was the best opportunity to extend my career. It worked out."

Of his 151 career victories, 118 came while he was wearing a Devils sweater.

DIFFICULT EXIT

Most guys who came through the system or pulled on a Devils sweater have fond recollections of their years in Jersey.

Neal Broten is one of the exceptions. Neal did not leave on good terms with Devils management.

"I don't even watch [hockey] anymore," Broten said. "It left a sour taste in my mouth."

It began in the autumn of 1996. Shortly before the season opened, Neal was told he would not be starting the season in New Jersey.

"I was totally surprised," Broten said. "I think I led the team in scoring in training camp."

Neal said he asked to be traded. According to Neal, Devils general manager Lou Lamoriello told him he would trade him to another team if he took a pay cut, to make a trade more feasible.

The saga finally ended on November 22, 1996. Neal was sent to Los Angeles in exchange for future considerations. Neal retired not long after that, bitter about the way his career had ended.

BUBBA AND THE KIDS

Everywhere John McMullen went, his dog Bubba followed. "He was the heart and soul of the team," McMullen said of his pet.

But every now and then, Bubba got himself in trouble. One December, John brought Bubba to the team's Christmas party at South Mountain Arena. The team had hired a magician to entertain the players' kids. One of his tricks involved a rabbit.

Players weren't the only ones to misbehave on the Devils. Even John McMullen's dog. Bubba, got into a few scrapes along the way.
Illustration courtesy of Holly Resch

The magician was pretty good. He had all the kids laughing. After his act ended, the rabbit disappeared. Not even the magician could find him.

Then Bubba came running out from beneath a table, a dead bunny dangling from his mouth. As the players started laughing, most of the kids were bawling their eyes out.

The next day, one of the boys set up yellow police tape in the locker room. Cordoned off by the tape was a chalk outline of that poor rabbit.

CZECH IT OUT

Through the 2006–07 season, only six guys in Devils history had scored 40 goals over an 82-game schedule.

There's John MacLean, Pat Verbeek, Claude Lemieux, Alexander Mogilny, and Brian Gionta. The sixth guy was a rookie back in 1997–98, just two years away from joining the 40-goal club.

Patrik Elias doesn't remember a lot of the details from his rookie season when he put up 18 goals and 19 assists. He does remember looking around the dressing room, trying to find anyone who could speak Czech.

"Petr [Sykora] and Bobby [Holik] were here," Elias said.

Did it help? "No question," Elias said. "Yeah. Bobby at the beginning didn't speak much, but we got him going over the years."

Patty quickly became a fan favorite in Jersey. A quick skater and a flashy scorer, he helped the Devils to two of their three Stanley Cup titles.

499 . . . 499 . . . 499 . . .

Man, did Dave Andreychuk get an earful from his family and friends on the way to the 500th goal of his NHL career. After he popped in No. 499, the Devils invited his family in to witness the milestone.

But No. 500 didn't come easy. His relatives made at least one road trip, waiting for Andreychuk to pop the puck over the line one more time. Andreychuk said they got to see four Devils games, and spent most of their free time politely ribbing him for stalling.

"It was only two weeks at 499," Andreychuk said. "But it felt like two months."

The inevitable was delayed, but still exciting when No. 500 finally arrived. On March 15, 1997, he popped in a rebound—how else would you expect Andreychuk to score?—in front of his relatives.

"I'm glad it happened at home," Andreychuk said.

It was a long journey from the day in October of 1982 when he scored the first goal of his career. Back then he was wearing a Buffalo Sabres sweater. The team he finished his career with in 2006, the Tampa Bay Lightning, did not even exist when he was a rookie.

A few years later, on November 23, 2002, Andreychuk scored No. 600. He knocked in a rebound at the Meadowlands—just four games after he picked up No. 599.

A UNIQUE INDIVIDUAL

On longer road trips—not the little pit stops in New York or Philadelphia—players inevitably find spare time on their hands. Some nap. Some hit the bar scene. When Bobby Holik was with the Devils, he'd usually be looking for some museum or other cultural point of interest that piqued his curiosity.

"I took the opportunity to see things and do things," Holik said. "Go to the library or the museum, read the newspaper, catch up on what's going on in the world. I enjoy that. It's my hobby on the road."

Off the ice, Bobby has never been your garden-variety hockey player. He grew up in what was then Czechoslovakia. His grandparents and parents were always encouraging him to learn something new.

For Holik, an extended stay in Washington, D.C. is a gift. He can hit the Smithsonian, visit the monuments, and take in some United States history.

"Maybe there's not as much now," Holik said, "but in the past, there was a lot of down time on the road. I try to better myself as a person when I'm not bettering myself as a hockey player. That's how I was brought up. I don't like to waste time. There's so much to learn, to be better at."

MORRISON SCORES

Brendan Morrison got his first start in New Jersey because the Devils were still in contract negotiations with John MacLean.

Morrison was in Albany on a Wednesday night when New Jersey general manager Lou Lamoriello called. Lou told him to drive down immediately and stay at a hotel near the Meadowlands.

What happened the next day—December 4, 1997—is still surreal to Morrison. He flew into Pittsburgh, where the Devils were playing that night, on owner John McMullen's private jet. He took a cab from the airport right to the morning skate in downtown Pittsburgh. And then that night, Morrison scored on a rebound in his first career NHL game, a 4–0 victory over the Penguins.

At the time, only five other rookie Devils had ever scored in their first NHL appearances.

"That's something I'll never forget," Morrison said.

ANYBODY SEEN MY TEETH?

After games, Ken Daneyko would put his teeth back in his mouth. He spent most of his 1,283-game career chasing the puck into corners, leaving his mouth an easy target for errant sticks or flying pucks.

As he got older, his smile inherited more and more gaps. "It happened gradually," Daneyko said.

He lost his first tooth in the early 1980s, when he got into a fight with Bob Probert. He took a slapshot to the mouth in San Jose, leaving three or four teeth stuck in his mouth guard. The last tooth he lost during his career vanished when a stick clipped him high.

"That was a part of hockey," Daneyko said. "I loved it back then. Not now. Back when I was playing, it was not really a big deal."

Kenny would come on television with us after games sometimes. Someone usually had to remind him to put his teeth in before the cameras started rolling. Some nights, usually when the Devils were on the road, Kenny would come back to the locker room and his teeth wouldn't be where he placed them before the game.

"I was famous for leaving them everywhere," Daneyko said. "One time I had to get them mailed from the trainer."

A few of his former teammates swear there were nights they saw Kenny digging through some garbage can in some visiting locker room, certain someone had mistakenly tossed them out.

TIME TO GO

Jacques Lemaire didn't want to hang around and wait for the pink slip. He wanted to leave Jersey on his terms.

On May 8, 1998, Jacques decided he'd had a good run with the Devils. It was someone else's turn.

"There were a lot of young players coming in," Lemaire said. "The old players—they gave me so much. I couldn't take the old guys and put them aside to train the kids.

"I felt at that time somebody [new] had to come in, and I thought I'd brought these guys the highest I could. I couldn't bring that team further."

He didn't see how he could possibly tell the veterans—the same guys who'd helped him win that first Cup as a coach—to make room for the new wave of talent.

"It's tough when you've got guys who are playing their heart out for you for five years, then you come in and say they're not good enough [anymore]," Lemaire said. "Now they won't play fifteen minutes, they're only going to play ten."

14

DIVING FOR DOLLARS

WRITTEN INTO SASHA LAKOVIC'S Devils contract were clauses designed to prevent him from drinking. Sasha was one of many hockey players who battled demons. But he insists he played by the rules when he was in New Jersey.

"I was supposed to attend AA meetings and not drink while I was there," Lakovic said.

One night the team was on the road for a game against Edmonton. A few of the boys decided to hang out at the bar at a Hooters restaurant in the West Edmonton Mall. Sasha didn't want to spar with temptation, so he went for a walk with Petr Sykora, Patrik Elias, Brendan Morrison, and one or two other teammates.

Sasha still doesn't remember which guy dared him—maybe Patrik, maybe Brendan—but he'll never forget the dare itself.

"I'll give you a couple hundred dollars if you jump inside the pool," one of his teammates said to him.

The pool was located right in the middle of the West Edmonton Mall. One section of it hosted a daily dolphin

Sasha Lakovic was not one to step down from a dare. *Illustration courtesy of Holly Resch*

show. Another section featured a submarine ride that was closed for repair.

As Sasha glanced around the mall and mulled over the decision, every single one of his buddies offered to pony up $200 to see him swan dive into the pool.

"I'll do it," Lakovic told them.

He stripped down to his shorts, then hopped in and out before any security guard took notice of the sopping-wet professional hockey player. "All of us were howling," Lakovic said.

The story got back to his other teammates, and it eventually got back to New Jersey general manager Lou Lamoriello. Sasha took plenty of heat for his stunt. In two seasons with the Devils, he suited up for just eighteen games.

"I guess you could say I didn't get any leeway there at all," Lakovic said.

OH, THAT'S MY SISTER'S CHEESESTEAK

The two tables were adjacent to each other. At one sat David Conte, Lou Lamoriello, and the rest of New Jersey's scouting department. At the other sat an eighteen-year-old kid named Scott Gomez and his family.

This was the 1998 NHL Entry Draft. Conte and the Devils scouting staff had had their eyes on "Gomer" for a long time. And with two picks in the first round, they were fairly confident they'd be able to bring him aboard.

During the draft, Gomer, like most kids in his shoes, sat and waited. After twenty-five players were chosen, Gomer was still available. With the No. 26 pick, the Devils took defenseman Mike Van Ryan. If New Jersey didn't pluck Gomer with its other pick (No. 27), he would fall into the second round.

"I walked by [Scott] and winked," Conte said. "Every player has his heart set [on going in the first round]. I don't know if he thought I was goofing on him or not."

Sure enough, Conte plugged Corner's name into New Jersey's computer and the Devils made him the final pick of the first round. Conte was happy to get both Van Ryan and Gomer. That is, until he stumbled upon the Gomez table a little later and caught the new draft pick with his hands wrapped around a large cheesesteak.

"I was going to say, 'You shouldn't be eating that kind of stuff,'" Conte said. "Before I said anything, he said, 'I'm holding it for my sister.'"

"We hoped he was a quick skater. At least he was a quick thinker."

THE OLD BASKETBALL COURT

In Canada, most kids find a pond or a river or some other frozen sheet of ice for pickup hockey games. John Madden found a nearby basketball court.

John's path to the National Hockey League was unconventional to say the least, even if he tries to downplay the obstacles he overcame at just about every turn.

"My life, the way I grew up man, wasn't that bad," Madden told the *Asbury Park Press* in 2003. His parents divorced when he was young, and John spent time living with both his father and then his mother.

The basketball court was not in the best area, but it was a place to play. A buddy's father would spray the court with water on winter afternoons so that the blacktop would freeze.

He never grew any taller than 5-foot-ll, a little on the small side for most aspiring hockey players. Despite his size, he accomplished a lot after joining the Devils.

On October 28, 2000, he scored four goals against the Pittsburgh Penguins. In 2000, he won his first Stanley Cup. In 2001, he won the Selke Award, given annually to the best defensive forward in the National Hockey League. In 2003, he won his second Stanley Cup. He was as tenacious as any player who has ever traipsed through the Devils locker room, quite possibly as tenacious as any player in the entire league.

Not bad for a guy who began his hockey career on a frozen basketball court.

FORGET IT, KID

Scott Gomez's first bad game came early in his rookie season. Claude Lemieux was upset with Gomez's performance and let Gomez know about it.

Gomer was sulking, just as any rookie would after a tough night. Randy McKay noticed right away. He walked right up to Gomer's locker and told him to forget about it.

"Kid, that's the secret of the game," McKay told Gomez. "You got eighty-two of these things. You're not going to play eighty-two great games. Now let's go. I'll take you out to dinner."

McKay was pretty good with the young guys. Not bad with the old guys either, actually.

"He kept the room loose for sure," said Dave Andreychuk, one of McKay's more veteran teammates.

THE "A" LINE

The most famous combination in Devils history involved three talented players: Patrik Elias, a young flashy scorer; Petr Sykora, a guy who had a lot of talent; and Jason Arnott, a big kid at center.

Devils coach Robbie Ftorek came up with the idea. Why not try putting the three together? On February 6, 1999, Ftorek brought them together. Before long, they became known as the "A" line.

"We played together for three months and it paid off," Elias said. "Those were fun times. Awesome. Not just our line, but the whole team. . . . We had fun at practices and made each other better. We knew we had a good team."

It wasn't one play or one game that made everything click. It just took practice.

"Over time you build confidence," Elias said. 'You build chemistry, then you find each other."

They started finding each other often that season. After they were put together, Patty scored nine goals and had 18 assists over the Devils' final thirty-two games that season. It was a sign of things to come: Patty scored 35 goals the following season and 40 the season after that.

"It builds your confidence," Elias said. "Obviously, Robbie gave me my first chance. I'm very grateful for that."

Brendan Morrison was having lunch with his wife, her sister, and his brother-in-law at a Manhattan restaurant when he learned his time in New Jersey was over.

Morrison's brother-in-law is Daryl Reaugh, a former NHL goalie who played for Edmonton and Hartford. Reaugh was doing a phone interview with a radio station in Toronto on March 14, 2000—the day of the NHL trade deadline. He asked the host if he'd heard any rumblings about possible trades.

"We just heard a rumor that [Alexander] Mogilny is going to Jersey for [Brendan] Morrison," Reaugh was told.

"Oh, that's funny," Reaugh said. "I'm having lunch with him right now."

Reaugh told Morrison what the host had just told him. Then Morrison's cell phone began ringing left and right, one friend after another telling him he was headed to Vancouver.

By 3 p.m., the deadline had passed but he still hadn't heard anything concrete from the Devils.

"I pulled into my driveway and got a call from Marie [Carnevale]," Morrison said. "She said 'Lou wants to talk to you.' I said, 'Hey I already know what's going on.'"

It worked out well for both sides. Morrison was born in Pitt Meadows, British Columbia. For him, this was a chance to play close to home. With Mogilny in New Jersey, the Devils went on to win the 2000 Stanley Cup. Morrison eventually wound up playing between Markus Naslund and Todd Bertuzzi, combining to form one of the best lines in hockey.

"I just felt as a player, I wasn't developing," Morrison told me. "I wasn't where I wanted to be. I was kind of turning my wheels. So I was happy [about the trade]."

REPLACING ROBBIE

You wouldn't change coaches 74 games deep into an 82-game regular season. Unthinkable, right? Not if you're asking Robbie Ftorek.

Robbie coached two seasons in New Jersey. He won 47 games his first season and piled up 105 points. Seventy-four games into Season No. 2, Robbie had New Jersey sitting on 95 points, holding down a record of 41–25–8.

And that's when Devils general manager Lou Lamoriello pulled the whistle from his neck. With only eight games left, Lou fired Robbie and moved Larry Robinson into the hot seat.

"It's hard replacing someone you admire," Robinson said.

Robbie was the guy who first showed Larry how to run a practice. Replacing him that late in the season felt a little like elbowing a close friend and then stealing his car keys.

"I have a lot of respect and admiration for Robbie and I like Robbie a lot," Robinson said. "He gave me a chance when I was first starting."

Larry was a welcome breeze in the dressing room. He was handed the reins under unusual circumstances, sure, but with eight games left, he didn't exactly have time to mull over the circumstances.

"I just wanted to get back to square one when I first started," Robinson said. "I wanted to play a little bit different. Robbie was more offensive-minded as far as the way he wanted to play the game."

It's not shocking that Larry, a Hall of Fame defenseman, stressed defense.

"Each coach has his own style," Robinson said. "Mine was a little bit more defensive. A lot like the way Jacques Lemaire ran his club."

With Larry at the helm, the Devils went just 4–4 over those final eight games. But it was his 16–7 mark during that postseason that everybody remembers.

"Once the playoffs get going, for the coach, it's tough," Robinson said. "You don't get a lot of breathing room. Once the first game's over, you're preparing for the second one, and once the second one's over, you're preparing for the third. Two and a half months were just like a blur. It was go, go, go, go."

By the time he saw a stop sign, his Devils had won their second Stanley Cup.

FIRE AND BRIMSTONE

Larry Robinson has never been the type of coach to beat players over the head with his vocal cords. In head coaching stints in both New Jersey and Los Angeles, Larry ran steady ships. He rarely yelled.

But when his Devils fell behind the Philadelphia Flyers three games to one during the 2000 Eastern Conference Finals, Larry exploded. Some of his players remember Larry throwing a garbage can. Was this the real Larry—mellow on the outside, fierce and intense on the inside—standing in front of them?

"I don't think it's something you can do every night," Robinson said. "It just happened. The timing was right and I think I caught them by surprise. They don't normally hear things like that coming from me."

Claude Lemieux was sitting in the postgame locker room that night, after the Devils dropped Game 4, 3–1, the team's third straight loss. Most Devils were trying to keep their surprise at Robinson's outburst to themselves. Not Claude Lemieux.

"I knew [Larry] as a player," Lemieux said. "I knew how emotional he could get when his button was pushed."

After the Devils took a 1–0 lead in the series, Philadelphia won Game 2 (4–3), Game 3 (4–2), and Game 4 (3–1). With the Devils one game away from heading home for the summer, Larry stormed into the locker room and yelled at his team for not playing to its potential, for not following the game plan.

"That's what upset me the most," Robinson said. "A lot of guys were taking it upon themselves to do things they wanted to do. They weren't listening to coaches. It's one of the reasons they got their butts kicked."

In a speech Larry said was "probably a little louder, a bit more animated," the Devils head coach lit into his players. Just about every player took it to heart.

"It was one of those times where you look back and say he was the greatest man you've ever met," said Bobby Holik, a forward on that team. "He coached from the bottom of his heart, nothing else. [That outburst] was a kick in the pants. He told you, 'Look in the mirror. You can do better than that for the team.'"

And then it happened. The Devils won Game 5 (4–1), Game 6 (2–1), and Game 7 (2–1). Devils captain Scott Stevens hammered Flyers forward Eric Lindros in Game 7, a hit that went a long way toward helping New Jersey capture the series.

New Jersey went on to win the Stanley Cup that season. Larry's players still point toward that speech as the difference.

"The way Larry came out and said that, and the way he was," Holik said, "he became an instant legend as a coach. He was already a legend as a player."

15

BEGINNER'S LUCK

LATE IN THE 2000 STANLEY CUP RUN, a kid from New Glasgow, Nova Scotia became a big part of the team for the first time. New to the Devils and new to the NHL, Colin White turned to two of the elder statesmen and his Hall of Fame coach for advice.

"Larry [Robinson], Scotty [Stevens], and Dano [Ken Daneyko]," White said. "Those three are all obviously considered great defensemen by a young kid [like me] coming in."

It was an incredible year for Whitey. As a late-season call-up, he played just 21 games during the regular season. Then when the playoffs started, Larry put him in the lineup for all 23 playoff games.

"I was so happy to be in the NHL," White said. "Once we kept going each round, I was like, 'Oh my, we're getting closer.' I guess I never realized how much work and effort went into winning the Cup. I just kind of stepped into that team."

Other guys may have gotten jitters during that playoff run. Whitey says he wasn't one of them.

"The first year I wasn't as nervous in the playoffs," White said, "just because I didn't really know what was at stake."

And the Devils just kept winning. With White in the line-up, New Jersey beat Florida, then Toronto, then Philadelphia, and then Dallas. A few months earlier, he'd been taking bus rides on road trips, and now here he was, skating around the rink, holding the Stanley Cup above his head.

"Playoffs are the best time of the year." White said. "That's what you play for. That's when hockey's fun. Everything's a challenge, every game means so much."

GOAL! GOAL!

By the end of the 2015–16 regular season, Patrik Elias had scored 408 goals during the regular season and 45 more during the postseason.

Two of those postseason strikes stand out more than all 408 of those regular-season goals and his 43 other playoff goals. His two goals against the Philadelphia Flyers during Game 7 of the 2000 Eastern Conference Finals headline his list of career highlights.

"They were the most important goals I've had in my career," Elias said.

The Devils actually trailed 3–1 that series. Patty was one loss away from heading back to Europe for the summer months.

The trip would have to wait. New Jersey won Games 5 and 6, before Patty played the hero in Game 7.

"During the first period on the power play," Elias said, "Bobby [Holik] gave it to me across. I was kind of on a break. I think I went five hole."

One goal wasn't going to be enough to topple Philly. As time ticked down, Patty followed Jason Arnott toward the net.

"Arnie fanned on the shot," Elias said. "I came behind . . . and put it in the net."

A few minutes later, the Devils were headed to their second Stanley Cup Finals.

"It doesn't come along that often," Elias said. "You're reminded of guys who have been there, done that so many times."

STILL PALS?

It's tough enough lining up against a former teammate in the playoffs. So imagine how hard it was for Colin White, who had to play against one of his boyhood friends during the 2000 Stanley Cup Finals.

Like most kids who grow up skating on ponds in Canada, Whitey began playing hockey almost as soon as he could skate. But there was another kid in New Glasgow, Nova Scotia who grew up with the same dream.

White played more than a few pick-up games against Jonathan Sim, a kid born just three months before him. The fact that Sim was on the Dallas Stars team that won the Stanley Cup in 1999 left White both proud and hungry.

"He had won the Stanley Cup the year before," White said. "I wasn't going to be satisfied going home without one. I was hoping for his success as an individual but mostly our team's success."

Their conversations during that series were limited.

"I think we talked before the round started," White said. "We said good luck to each other, and that was it."

White gave the town of New Glasgow a second son to celebrate that postseason. White's Devils beat Sim's Stars four games to two.

After it ended, they resumed talking to each other.

"THE SON I NEVER HAD"

Only the security lights were still on when Martin Brodeur and Jacques Caron slipped back out onto the ice at Reunion Arena. This was hours after Stanley Cup No. 2 for Marty, well after most of his teammates had disappeared to one party or another.

The star and his coach, joined by Marty's family, wandered over toward the net where he was standing when Jason Arnott scored the game-winner down the opposite end.

Marty was happy. Just not quite as happy as his goalie coach.

"Marty's a very special person to me," Caron said. "I never had a son. He's the son I never had."

Marty goes out of his way to surprise Jacques with gifts after some of his grandest accomplishments. After Marty led Canada to the gold medal at the 2002 Winter Olympics, he had rings made for both Jacques and his father Denis. He got Jacques a brand new car after winning one Cup, bought him a Rolex after another.

"This guy is very appreciative," Caron said. "He's not a selfish type of person."

One of Jacques' favorite punch lines is the one he saves for when people ask him what makes a good goaltending coach. "A good goaltender," Caron jokes.

THAT MARTIN BRODEUR CALM

On Claude Lemieux's short list of the top goalies in NHL history, he has Patrick Roy at No. 1 and Martin Brodeur at No. 2.

Dr. John McMullen, the man who brought professional hockey to New Jersey, poses with the Stanley Cup on July 31, 2000. *AP Images*

"That's how I rate it so far," Lemieux said midway through Marty's playing career. "When Marty retires, it might be a different story."

The one thing Claude loved about Marty—what most guys love about Marty—is how calm he is on game days. Take it from me: Goalies can be head cases the mornings they have big games. But Marty never seemed nervous.

"If Marty's not dressed, you wouldn't know whether he was playing or not," Lemieux said.

THE PARKING LOT

After the first two Stanley Cups, the team held parades in the parking lot at the Meadowlands. The team's supporters took quite a beating from New York Rangers and New York Islanders fans, all of whom had a good laugh over a group of players parading around on asphalt.

"The parking lot thing that went on is great," said longtime season-ticket holder Ray Henry. "I think it's better than any parade could be."

"It started in the morning," Henry said. "Regular people got there and tailgated. . . . You partied from lunchtime until 10 o'clock at night. It went on and on. They had a stage and you met all the players. I think that's much better than going down Broadway. Even if they dropped tickertape, it's over as soon as they pass."

TAXI!

The night that Scott Gomez received the Calder Trophy as the NHL's Rookie of the Year went smoothly. It was the following day that everything turned chaotic.

In Toronto for the NHL Awards ceremony, Gomer walked up to the stage and accepted the award from Christopher Reeve. Gomer had scored 19 goals and had 51 assists that season, helping the Devils to their second Cup title that June.

Honored to receive the award, Gomer's toughest challenge was making it back home from Toronto.

"I'll never forget," Gomez said. "I missed my flight. Dano [Ken Daneyko] was supposed to come get me. He never got me. I took the next flight out of Toronto and ended up at LaGuardia."

When he got there, the line for cabs was wrapped all around the complex. A complete stranger tapped Gomer on the shoulder and told him he might have better luck catching a cab upstairs where taxis were dropping off people for departing flights.

Illegal, maybe. But Gomer was exhausted. He just wanted to get home.

"The cab ride was like 100 bucks," Gomez said. "Dead heat, it was maybe 100 degrees outside. All I wanted to do was get home and rest all day."

A few seconds after he walked in to his place, his phone was ringing. Jay Pandolfo, one of Gomer's closest friends on the team, was on the other end of the line.

"I got us plane tickets," Pandolfo told Gomez. "We're going to Boston today."

SELLING THE DRAMA

During the early '90s, rumors circulated daily about whether the team would be staying put in New Jersey. John McMullen threatened to move the Devils to Nashville, Tennessee, long before the Nashville Predators took up residence down there.

"We were definitely going to do it," McMullen said. "Finally they came around. But it was really close. Am I sorry [we didn't leave]? No way. I'm so happy we stayed."

John never moved the team, but he eventually had to sell it. He held out until the price he was offered made it impossible to say no.

"They kept after me," McMullen said. "They offered $100 million, then $125, then $150. Finally they got to $175."

McMullen picked up his phone shortly after that offer went on the table and found NBA commissioner David Stern on the other end of the line.

"He called me and said, 'You ought to take it,'" McMullen said. "'That's a good number.'"

Not long after that, John McMullen, the man who had helped bring hockey to New Jersey, was handing his team over to someone else.

16

SMALL, BUT STRONG

AT 5-FOOT-7, BRIAN GIONTA was one of the smallest players to ever wear a Devils jersey. He scored a school-record 123 goals during his four years at Boston College and was the center-piece of a team that won a national title his senior year. But Gionta was short. And teams are wary of drafting and dressing tiny players, fearing they'll get run over or stomped by the big boys.

Yet all it took was 37 games in Albany before he was called up to the Devils.

"You're always waiting for it and wondering," Gionta said. "But you never know when it's going to come. And when I got it, I was obviously very excited. That's what you dream of as a kid, to finally get the phone call and get a chance to make it happen."

A lot of guys have hit Brian Gionta since he made the team in 2001. Gionta jokes that he remembers the first hit, but not the guy who hit him.

"He hit me too hard," Gionta said.

Rob Blake knocked him silly one game. The hardest one I remember was at Madison Square Garden, when New York Rangers forward Eric Lindros absolutely killed him.

"You try to get right back up obviously," Gionta said. "You try not to show that it hurt or anything. But you don't want to go right off either, because that kind of shows you might be hurting, too."

He's a tough one, alright. Lou Lamoriello took a chance when he drafted Gionta in 1998, and the chance paid off beautifully.

In 2006, Gionta set the Devils' single-season goals record with 48.

HE GIVETH, HE TAKETH AWAY

Ken Daneyko was a good guy, but not much of a goal scorer. Those rare nights when he did score, everyone in the locker room heard about it. Kenny would stomp around the locker room screaming, "Three! Sixty-six! Ninety-nine!" to any team-mate willing to listen.

Kenny wore No. 3. The other two numbers he'd yell belonged to Mario Lemieux and Wayne Gretzky, two of the greatest goal scorers the game has ever seen. He'd use the phrase, "Between the three of us" to open conversations about his goal-scoring prowess, adding his 36 career goals to whatever their totals happened to be at the time.

One night when the Devils were playing in Anaheim, the puck found its way onto Kenny's stick and Kenny found himself on a breakaway. He went top shelf, sending a rocket into the back of the cage.

"Nicest goal he ever scored in his career," said Scott Niedermayer, one of Daneyko's partners back on the blue line.

At the next stoppage, the on-ice officials halted the game and called up for video replay. Just before Kenny scored, Anaheim's Steve Thomas ripped a puck so hard that it blitzed right through the back netting. After looking at the replay, officials credited Thomas with a goal, then scrolled back the clock and wiped out everything that happened after the Thomas goal.

Everything. Including Kenny's pretty goal.

I'll bet Mario and Wayne were breathing a little easier after that. For the moment, their records were safe.

STILL STINGS

The 1994 conference finals loss to the New York Rangers hurt. The 2004 first-round exit to the Philadelphia Flyers didn't go down easy, either. But the defeat that still gnaws at Lou Lamoriello is that loss to the Colorado Avalanche in the 2001 Stanley Cup Finals.

"To this day," Lamoriello said, "it bothers me. I look back [and think] maybe I could have done something differently, or maybe I could have handled things a little bit differently. To this day, that loss bothers me as much as any loss we've had."

His team was up 3–2 in the series. Game 6 was a home game. Then the Devils went 0-for-2, two absolutely crushing setbacks in Lou's eyes.

"In '94, we were still growing," Lamoriello said. "We were still learning. When you're experienced, when you have some history, you can't accept it, whereas you can accept things when there is that inexperience in everybody."

ONE MORE CHANCE

The end of the 2000–01 season still doesn't sit well with many players who were on that Devils team. Up 3–2 against the Colorado Avalanche in the Stanley Cup Finals, one game away from winning back-to-back titles, New Jersey lost Games 6 and 7 and went home empty-handed.

During the 2002–03 Cup run, New Jersey goalie Martin Brodeur said he would not change a thing about the way he prepared for that Game 7. Larry Robinson, the coach of that team, looks back and sees a lot he would have done differently.

"I made two mistakes," Robinson said. "No. 1, when we came back from Colorado after Game 5, I should have brought all the players to a hotel so they couldn't go back and see all their friends and have their friends tell them how great they were. The guys began thinking they didn't have to do the same things they did in Game 5. I made a mistake there."

The other thing he wishes he could go back and erase are his personnel choices for the final two games of the series. Larry inserted Jason Arnott even though Arnie was coming off an injury.

"Jason Arnott had been hurt," Robinson said. "I think we brought him back in because of the 'A' line and everything else. I don't think he was ready to play. [Sergei] Nemchinov was there and had played really, really well on the same line."

Game 6 final score: Colorado 4, New Jersey 0.

Game 7 final score: Colorado 3, New Jersey 1.

BREAKING UP IS HARD TO DO

It had to end. As quickly as the "A" line began striking fear in opponents, it was taken apart. First on the ice, then off the ice.

Scott Niedermayer helped the Devils win three Stanley Cups during his tenure in New Jersey. *Bruce Bennett Studios/Getty Images*

"When Larry [Robinson] came in," said Patrik Elias, the left wing on the line, "we were still playing well and everything. The next year, we didn't play as well as we could. He made changes, started switching the lines. That was pretty much the end."

All three players—Elias, Jason Arnott, and Petr Sykora—enjoyed some of the best seasons of their careers when they were playing together. Patty had a 35-goal, 37-assist season in 1999–2000. Sykie put up 25 goals and 43 assists that same year.

Arnie was the first to go. At the 2001–02 National Hockey League trade deadline, Devils general manager Lou Lamoriello made Arnie the centerpiece of a trade that brought Joe Nieuwendyk and Jamie Langenbrunner to New Jersey. That summer, Lou made the breakup complete, moving Sykora to Anaheim.

"It was our fault in a way," Elias said. "Maybe we took it for granted. We didn't work as hard as we should have. We didn't work on ourselves. You've got to really practice every time."

MOM DRIVES AND DAD HOLDS THE WHISTLE

Soccer matches. Hockey games. Name a sport, and Christian Berglund's parents were there. His mother, Christina, would drive him all over the place. His father, Lars-Goran, was actually one of his first coaches.

They both got called on a Monday afternoon, not long after Berglund got a call of his own. When New Jersey's minor-league club, the Albany River Rats, won back-to-back games one weekend, Devils general manager Lou Lamoriello decided to bring Berglund up for the first time.

"I think we only won back-to-back games once in Albany [that season]," Berglund said.

On January 9, 2002, he was in the lineup for a game against Calgary. Mom made it to the game. Dad made it to the game. A whole handful of Berglunds were there, cheering for New Jersey.

The Devils didn't disappoint. They won 5–1 that night. And Bergie had an assist in front of his parents.

"It was probably the best moment so far," Berglund said during the 2003–04 season, not long before he was traded to the Florida Panthers.

Bergie didn't last too long in New Jersey. But at least his parents were there for Game No. 1, when he first cracked the lineup.

"It was fun to let them see this moment with me," Berglund said. "It made everything better. Of course, it was a dream come true."

YOU'RE FIRED

I don't know if I've ever been more surprised than I was the moment I heard Larry Robinson was fired during the 2001–02 season. In two postseasons, Larry took the Devils to two Stanley Cup Finals and one Stanley Cup title.

He had it all as a player. He had it all as a coach. I played for Al Arbour, one of the true all-time legends, and I've told Larry I thought he was closer in style to Al than anyone I've ever met. But on January 28, 2002, Devils general manager Lou Lamoriello replaced Larry with Kevin Constantine.

"If I had to do it over again," Robinson said, "I would have probably asked Lou to hang tight. We would have turned things around."

Larry thinks that two straight runs to the Finals may have drained some of the energy from his team.

"We just hit a low," Robinson said. "We weren't tired physically. We were more tired mentally. I think if we just backed off a little bit, allowed them to regain some of their composure, we would have turned it around."

Larry handled the firing the way he handles everything: with pure class. He was humble enough to return to the Devils as an assistant coach, a move most former head coaches couldn't fathom.

Some days he'd catch himself offering advice to a young player that ran contrary to what Kevin was teaching. Those moments, he'd back off and tell that player to go by what Kevin said.

"I did it more because of my respect for Lou and the organization than anything else," Robinson said. "He'd been very good to me since I'd been there. He gave me the opportunity to coach. He thought enough of my abilities to put me in charge."

NEW SCENERY

Almost every player dreads getting that call. You're enjoying life in one city on one day and you're traded to another city the next.

It wasn't like that for Jeff Friesen. He had some of his best seasons out in San Jose, before he wound up in Anaheim.

Anaheim was rough—a great city, but not a kind place for Jeff. After 96 games over parts of two seasons with the Mighty Ducks, he was almost expecting the call saying he was being shipped elsewhere.

"I thought I might get traded at the [NHL] draft," Friesen said.

The draft came and went, and Jeff was still a Duck. He didn't know what to think anymore. Maybe Anaheim liked him more than he knew.

"I thought maybe I'd get another shot there," Friesen said.

Then on July 6, Lou Lamoriello tweaked the franchise. He shipped longtime Devils forward Peter Sykora to the Mighty Ducks as part of a trade that brought Jeff east.

"I was excited when I heard I got traded," Friesen said. "First thing you think is Martin Brodeur, Scott Stevens, and Scott Niedermayer. And then guys like [John] Madden and [Colin] White. Those guys have been there and done it. You know you're going to have a chance to win it all."

Jeff said he felt like a rookie his first few months in Jersey, even though he had been in the NHL for eight seasons. Joe Nieuwendyk made it easy for him.

"He was great to me," Friesen said. "He helped me fit in right away. And I got a chance to play with him."

With Joe centering his line, Jeff's career was reborn. By the end of the season, he had scored the game-winning goal in Game 7 of the Eastern Conference Finals and two more goals in Game 7 of the Stanley Cup Finals.

A WALL STREET COMMODITY

In the back of his mind, Bobby Holik always knew hockey was about dollars and cents. Any doubt he had was squashed back in 1992, when he was traded from the Hartford Whalers to the New Jersey Devils.

'You realize it's a business early on in your career," Holik said. "I was twenty-one. Up to that point, I played and it was fun—we had great times. But you're a commodity, and they can trade you around the way they want."

When it was Bobby's turn to strike back at the system, he took full advantage. He became a free agent during the summer of 2002. Not only did he leave, not only did he get a boatload of money, but he went to the New York Rangers—the same Rangers he battled so ferociously during his 724-game run with the Devils.

Over the span of a few seasons, Bobby went from playing on the Crash Line to playing on the Cash Line.

"Unfortunately—a big emphasis on unfortunately—it had to come to this," Holik said. "I had a great ride in New Jersey for ten years, but it was time to move on for several reasons. So I moved on."

The season after Bobby signed with the Blueshirts, the Devils won their third Stanley Cup. They missed him, sure, but they managed just fine without him.

17

MATCHING DEFENSEMEN

WHEN PAT BURNS joined the Devils before the 2002–03 season, New Jersey began matching lines as often as any team in the league. If Tampa Bay Lightning coach John Tortorella sent Martin St. Louis and his linemates out onto the ice, Burns usually countered with his best checking forwards and his top defensive pairing. Usually that meant Scott Stevens would be out there patrolling the ice, ready to hammer any forward who dared cross the blue line.

By the time Pat came to town, Scotty was used to this type of strategy. He remembers Jacques Lemaire introducing it to the guys when he first arrived in Jersey.

"He's one of the best at putting people in a position to succeed," Stevens said. "He knew we weren't a real high-powered team [in 1995]. We had to work with what we had.

"It was unheard of—putting the top two defensemen against the best offensive guys. Now it's something almost every team does."

During that 2003 Stanley Cup playoff run, Scotty spent most of his shifts playing alongside Brian Rafalski. Brian's quick. He moves the puck really well. Playing with Scotty that season, he helped the Devils lead the league in fewest goals allowed.

"It's always fun to try to frustrate the other team's top forwards, to not give up any goals," Stevens said. "If we could keep the top line off the board, we had a great chance of winning."

PIE, COLIN?

As birthday presents go, the one the boys gave Colin White on his twenty-fifth birthday wasn't very good. Don't expect Whitey to forget it—it was more of a prank than a present.

"Everyone was in on it, that's for sure," White said.

The boys really gave it to Whitey, catching him unaware during a practice in Columbus, Ohio during the 2002–03 season. Pat Burns called his team into a huddle in the middle of the ice. Whitey followed his teammates over toward Burns.

One player was missing, but Whitey barely noticed.

"Dog [John Madden] skated over to the bench," White said. "I obviously wasn't paying attention to what he was doing."

When Madden skated back toward the huddle, he had a shaving-cream pie in his hands. He crept over toward Whitey, then let him have it. Splat! Right in Whitey's face.

"Actually, it went more in my ear," White said. "And my gear smelled like shaving cream the next three or four games."

It could have been worse. It could have been apple pie.

RUPP'S TWO-GOAL DEBUT

The dressing room was empty, only a few equipment guys scurrying around, when Mike Rupp showed up at the

Meadowlands for his first day on the job in the NHL. He didn't want to make a bad impression, so he asked about five different guys what time he was supposed to get to the arena.

Not nervous, but maybe a little paranoid, Mike got there about an hour before the first of the Devils veterans walked into the room.

Rupper had played a minor-league game in Albany on a Sunday afternoon. After the game, Albany coach Dennis "Red" Gendron called him into his office. This was it, Red told him. He'd gotten the call.

Mike, his wife, Christie, and the couple's young daughter, Madeline, hopped in a car and made the trip down to Jersey. None of them were ready for the fireworks that followed.

On Mike's first shift, he got hit. Florida forward Peter Worrell offered his welcome by slamming Rupp down onto the ice with an elbow.

"It was a good wake-up call," Rupp said.

It helped him settle down. He would be laughing minutes later, when he put the puck in the net.

But officials disallowed the goal. No big deal, right? Mike still got his first NHL goal that night, converting a feed from Jim McKenzie.

"Nobody came to me," Rupp said. "So I just kind of glided in. Then I shot it. I remember shooting it far side, just trying to get it off quick, and I put it over [Roberto] Luongo's shoulder."

And then the nice debut turned into a dream debut, maybe the best opening act by any Devils player in team history. Mike scored again, this time on a 2-on-1 with Jay Pandolfo.

One night. Two goals. "It let me know that I could play," Rupp said. "And it made me feel a little more comfortable."

ROOKIE LUCK

Every guy in the locker room gets ripped apart by a coach somewhere along the line, some more than others. One game during Mike Rupp's rookie campaign, he had Devils coach Pat Burns screaming one minute and laughing the next.

It was February, about a month after Mike had made the team for the first time, and New Jersey was playing in Phoenix. Mike was sitting on the bench as Burns quickly cycled one line after another on and off the ice.

Mike came up as a center, but Burns had him playing on Scott Gomez's wing that night. When Burns wanted a certain line out on the ice, he would call out the last name of the line's centerman, and all three guys were supposed to head out there.

"Gomez," Burns yelled.

Scott hopped the boards, but poor Mike forgot he was playing wing, not center. Burns looked out, counted his guys, realized he was playing down a man.

"Who's supposed to be out there?" he yelled.

Mike realized a split second later he was supposed to be out there. He hustled out, took two strides, slipped behind a Phoenix defenseman, and scored.

The Devils won the game 3–0. Mike's goal stood up as the game-winner.

"I was too nervous to celebrate," Rupp said. When he got back to the bench, the entire team was laughing at him. Even Burns.

CHASING THE BUS

Grant Marshall was with the Devils for less than two months when they tried leaving for a playoff game without him.

Just before Game 5 of New Jersey's 2003 Eastern Conference semifinal series with the Tampa Bay Lightning, Marshall came down from his hotel room at 4:30 p.m. The bus wasn't scheduled to leave until 4:45 p.m. for the short ride over to the Meadowlands.

"We usually have a snack," Marshall said, "and then get on the bus."

But when he got down to the lobby, he spotted the bus already taking off. Marshall glanced down at his watch: 4:30 p.m. Something wasn't right.

"I rushed out the door with my bags," Marshall said. "I had to go up a hill, but finally got to the bus."

According to Marshall, Devils coach Pat Burns blamed assistant coach John MacLean. Johnny Mac was in charge of counting up the guys to make sure everybody was there.

Things worked out for Marshall, and they worked out even better for the Devils once they stopped and let him on the bus. The Devils and Lightning went to triple overtime that night. The game finally ended when—guess who?—Grant Marshall scored the game-winner to clinch the series and send the Devils into the Eastern Conference Finals against the Ottawa Senators.

As the game rolled into the first overtime, Marshall said he remembers this image jumping through his head: he wanted to be the guy to score the game-winning goal, then disappear underneath a pile of teammates.

"I was really hoping to get the puck and get the goal for the guys," Marshall said, "and have them cheering and going crazy."

Before that season, Marshall had played in six postseasons and won a Stanley Cup with the Dallas Stars. But he didn't have a single playoff goal on his playoff resume.

That postseason Marshall scored six times, a nice complement to New Jersey's other forwards as the team raced toward its third Stanley Cup in franchise history.

DON'T I KNOW YOU?

You think *your* mom had it tough? How about Carol Niedermayer? The poor woman had to watch one son go head to head with the other with the Stanley Cup hanging in the balance.

It happened in the 2003 Stanley Cup Finals, when Scott Niedermayer's Devils met up with Rob Niedermayer's Anaheim Mighty Ducks. So many reporters wanted to talk to Mrs. Niedermayer that New Jersey's public relations staff actually set up a conference call for her.

"Scotty has won two," Carol said two days before Game 1 of those Finals. "Robbie hasn't won one. I'll be cheering for both of them, but ultimately I would like to see the Ducks win the Stanley Cup."

Fourteen days after Carol said that, Scott won his third Stanley Cup. Rob was left looking for his first.

"We'll remember the experience," Niedermayer said, "It'll be special down the road. At the time, it was a little tough."

They didn't cut off the lines of communication during the series, the way some brothers might, but they didn't talk hockey. Scott and Rob found other things to fill the gaps. Scott said it may have been easier had they both won Cups heading into the series.

"It would have relieved a lot of the difficulties of the series," Niedermayer said. "Maybe we could have just enjoyed it."

Both players had solid series, and I know several writers had Scott near the top of their Conn Smythe ballots for the Most Valuable Player of the postseason. Maybe wanting to beat the other stirred passions in both players.

"It was the kind of attitude we had when we were eight, ten, and twelve years old," Niedermayer said. "We wanted to beat each other at all costs."

There is a happy ending. In 2007, Scott and Rob won the Stanley Cup together, helping Anaheim win its first title in franchise history.

SWEET EXHAUSTION

The night before Game 7 of the 2003 Stanley Cup Finals, the Devils were required to make one more media appearance before game day.

They'd lost Game 6 5–2 in Anaheim. They'd hopped off a cross-country flight earlier in the afternoon, then driven over to the hotel near the Meadowlands. Most of the guys were dragging. But what sweet exhaustion, knowing you could be carrying the Stanley Cup around the ice the following night.

"As an athlete," said Devils forward Jeff Friesen, "it's a dream day. Every breath you take, it's just like time standing still. All those hours in the gym, all the stuff you go through during the course of the year, your career, the pressure, people doubting you—everything.

"You can grab the Stanley Cup in one game. I wish every day could be like that."

Especially the way things worked out for Jeff the following day. He tried to follow his usual routines, but they didn't come easy. Jeff tried to block out everything until the opening face-off.

"It's just not your normal day when you wake up," Friesen said.

HAPPILY EVER AFTER

Did your heart jump when they announced the scratches for Game 7 of the 2003 Stanley Cup Finals and Ken Daneyko wasn't one of them? Devils coach Pat Burns had scratched

Kenny during the first six games of that series, as New Jersey and the Anaheim Mighty Ducks batded all the way to a seventh game.

The night before Game 7, Burns called Kenny over and told him he was putting him in for Game 7.

"I thought I should have been playing anyway," Daneyko said. "I think 99 percent of people did too. But I'm a believer it happened for a reason."

The Devils won Game 7 3–0. The crowd chanted "DAN-O, DAN-O" every time Kenny got his stick on the puck. He'd won two other Cups in New Jersey, but this one had an entirely different feel to it.

"For me," Daneyko said, "it was kind of the perfect ending."

He would retire from the game about a month later at a farewell press conference that was as emotional as that night in Game 7.

"I had a couple calls," Daneyko said. "Token calls from teams, possibly signing or coming to camp. I really didn't entertain the idea. I wasn't coming back to New Jersey. It was just the way I wanted it to end."

He loved labeling himself as a "lunch pail guy" that New Jersey fans could relate to. Kenny insists he probably knew about two-thirds of the fans who had attended Game 7.

The arena seats 19,040 for hockey games. By Kenny's estimate, he knew 12,693 of those fans. Seems high, but Kenny does know a lot of people. Maybe that's why the cheers resonated so loudly that final night of his career.

"Some people have storybook endings," Daneyko said. "Mine ended up the old Cinderella, happily ever after, as far my career went."

GAME 7 HERO

They ushered Mike Rupp to one interview after another as the clock inched toward midnight after Game 7 of the 2003 Stanley Cup Finals. Mike, just twenty-three at the time and with only 26 regular-season games on his NHL resume, was the hero.

The Devils and Mighty Ducks had won three games apiece heading into the night.

Mike was in the lineup, a dream come true for a kid out of Cleveland, Ohio. Yet there he was, charging at Anaheim goalie Jean Sebastien-Giguere with the game tied 0–0. Scott Niedermayer kept the puck in the zone and flipped it toward Giguere.

"All I was trying to do was get to the net," Rupp said.

Mike got there, tipping it past the goalie to put the Devils ahead 1–0. Martin Brodeur shut Anaheim's scorers out that night, giving Mike the title of "Stanley Cup hero."

He was numb. When he finally came off the ice, he told reporters to check back with him in a couple days. Maybe it would all have sunken in by then and he'd have better answers.

18

THE NORRIS: SO CLOSE, SO FAR

THREE STANLEY CUPS, but no Norris Trophy.

A Conn Smythe Trophy, but no Norris Trophy.

A Hall of Fame career, but no Norris Trophy.

Scott Stevens entered the 2004–05 season carrying the label of the best defenseman to ever play the game who had never won the Norris Trophy—a label that stuck whether he wanted it or not.

"I guess that's as close as you can be to being the Norris Trophy winner," Stevens said. "I guess by winning the Stanley Cup three times, it's taken some of the pressure off. I don't dwell on it."

The Norris, voted on annually by members of the Professional Hockey Writers Association, is given annually to the league's top defenseman. By the end of the 2003–04 season, Scotty had been voted onto fourteen all-star teams. You'd think one of those seasons would have been good enough to net him one of the highest honors an NHL defenseman can receive.

"I've always approached the regular season as trying to be the best I can at my position," Stevens said. "That's all the motivation I used. I try to be an all-star and go from there."

One season was more frustrating than all the others. During the Devils' 1993–94 campaign, Scotty led the squad in scoring with 78 points. His plus-minus rating was a staggering plus-53.

"[I thought] that was the year I was going to win it," Stevens said.

When the ballots came in, Ray Borque had edged Scotty by just four votes. It was the second time he'd finished No. 2 behind Borque.

THE HITTING

Scott Stevens always liked football growing up in Canada. Surprise, surprise. There's a lot of hitting in football, and when Scotty's out there on the ice, there's a lot of hitting in hockey.

"I was always physical," Stevens said. "I always played physical as a young player. It was part of my game."

Even after winning three Stanley Cups and hovering as a perennial candidate to win the Norris Trophy, Scotty will be best remembered for his hits. John Davidson put out a book called *Hockey for Dummies* a few years back. Inside, he listed Scotty as one of the ten best hitters in NHL history.

That makes perfect sense to me. If you ever hear the names Eric Lindros, Slava Kozlov, and Paul Kariya in the same sentence, you can bet the topic of conversation has something to with Stevens and his hitting.

All three guys (Kozlov in 1995, Lindros in 2000, Kariya in 2003) were on the receiving end of monster shots that Scotty unleashed during playoff games. All three just happened to be seasons when the Devils went on to win the Stanley Cup.

Coincidence? Probably not.

But don't think Scotty doesn't fret over the guys he's planted: "Pretty much all the times you hit someone and they don't get up, you're always worried," Stevens said. "It doesn't matter whether they're on your team or not."

LIFE OF A SCOUT

Scouts have it rough. Most scouts are away from home for long stretches at a time. Most scouts rack up plenty of miles on their cars. Jan Ludvig said that on average, he attends about six games a week and 150 to 180 games a season.

"I'd get yelled at by truckers," Ludvig said. "I'd drive at night, through mountains, and semis would try to blow me off the road."

Jan, one of three members of New Jersey's pro scouting staff during the 2003–04 season, spent several years scouting western Canada and the western half of the United States. He'd heard stories of avalanches blocking roads in the Rocky Mountains, so he tried a rather unorthodox method of preventing a breakdown.

According to Jan, he had a 500-liter gas tank installed in case he ever did get caught in the snow.

"If I ever get buried in an avalanche," Ludvig joked, "I can idle for about four months. They'll find me in the spring."

I asked Jan if he was worried that a tank that size could go up in flames if he ever got in a serious accident.

"Then it's going to be quick," Ludvig joked. "No one's going to know who was in that car."

WHERE'S THE PARISE JERSEY?

As part of their preparations for each summer's NHL Entry Draft, the Devils pack a few team jerseys to present to the players they're going to select in the first few rounds. They bring letters too, the kind they can slap onto the back of those jerseys just before they make their pick, so that a new guy gets his name on the back of his first Devils jersey.

There are too many players available for David Conte, New Jersey's director of scouting, to bring every kid's name. But by draft day, he usually has a pretty good grasp on the handful of players New Jersey might take.

Zach Parise threw a monkey wrench into the works.

"He was the first guy we did not have a name for," Conte said. "We didn't think he would be available. All of a sudden it had become a possibility."

The Devils had the twenty-second pick in the 2003 NHL Entry Draft, way too low to pick a guy like Zach. He was a star at the University of North Dakota. His father J.P. had played in the NHL. The Devils figured that by the time No. 22 rolled around, Zach would be long gone.

For some reason, he was still around when the Edmonton Oilers were picking at No. 17. New Jersey general manager Lou Lamoriello didn't hesitate. He packaged New Jersey's twenty-second and sixty-eighth overall picks and sent them to the Oilers in exchange for No. 17. And then the Devils grabbed Zach.

"We were really happy to have a crack at somebody who embodies a lot of those [positive] things," Conte said. "He's a

---

Scott Stevens, one of the most ferocious hitters in hockey history, crashes into Pittsburgh forward Konstantin Koltsov during a 2–1 Devils win in 2003. *Jason Cohn/Reuters/Landov*

guy who really wants to play, wants to fight for every inch of the ice. [We loved] his work ethic and competitiveness."

They loved him, but that didn't mean his jersey had his name on it.

IN VLADIMIR'S MEMORY

Back home in Russia, Vladimir Brylin taught his son Sergei how to play hockey: stick-handling, checking, just about everything. It was a real thrill for Vladimir to see his son eventually make a living in the National Hockey League.

Sergei did more than just make a living. In 2007, only five players could brag that they played for all three Devils teams that won Stanley Cups. Sergei is the guy who usually gets overlooked when he's grouped with Martin Brodeur, Scott Stevens, Scott Niedermayer, and Ken Daneyko.

I remember Sergei walking around the locker room with his right arm in a sling after a regular-season game in Washington during the 2002–03 season. In the weeks that followed, player after player bemoaned Sergei's absence, insisting they'd be a better team when he returned to the lineup.

Sergei made it back in time for the playoffs. And the Devils went on to win the Stanley Cup in June. It was a great year, until he got that phone call in September.

On September 23, 2003, Sergei's father died. Sergei scored the game-tying goal on the night the Devils raised their third banner to the rafters the following month. But all Sergei could think about was his father.

"It's hard," Brylin told reporters that night, fighting off a steady stream of tears. "It comes and goes. I guess it's going to take a long time to realize what happened."

CHAPTER 18

THE FEEL-GOOD STORY

There are hundreds of players whose dreams carry them into the American Hockey League, but leave them just short of the National Hockey League. For a long time, Rob Skrlac was one of those players.

Rob's a tough guy, a fighter. When a hockey coach needs someone to mix it up, Rob's the guy he usually sends out there.

He became a fan favorite in Albany, a city where he spent seven seasons toiling away, hoping someone would see something special in him and give him a shot with the big boys.

"After seven years in the minors, it starts going through your head," Skrlac told the *Asbury Park Press* in 2003. "Maybe it's not going to happen. Maybe it's time to focus on my next career."

Rob almost quit the game in 2003, almost shuttled off applications to various universities. He made one last call to the Devils. No promises, they told him, but why don't you come to training camp?

That December, he finally made it to the big time. On December 13, 2003, Rob played one shift, logging just twenty-three seconds of ice time. The key word is "played."

"I can tell my grandkids I played in the NHL," Skrlac said in 2003. "Not a lot of my friends can say that. Not a lot of guys in the world have played at the top level. Whether you play twenty-three seconds or twenty-three minutes, you're on the score sheet."

A few nights after his debut, the story got even better. Rob was setting a screen in front of the Atlanta Thrashers net when the puck bounced off his knee and into the cage. Believe it or not, it was the game-winning goal in a 3–0 Devils victory.

"In my second shift in the NHL, the puck bounced off my leg into the net," Skrlac told reporters that night. "What else can I ask for?"

167

Not much. It may have taken a while, but once Rob's dream came true, all those bus rides and hotel rooms in the minors were worth it.

NEED SOME PUCKS?

The morning of the 2004 NHL trade deadline, Tommy Albelin was sitting at his locker, removing his equipment after a morning skate.

If anybody was certain to be on the same team after the deadline passed, it was Tommy. He would turn forty in May. He showed up at training camp unsigned, playing on a tryout basis. His value to the Devils was much higher than what it would bring on the open market.

Devils coach Pat Burns liked Tommy because the thirty-nine-year-old defenseman could sit for weeks at a time, then hop into the lineup and play a great game.

Reporters loved his sense of humor. One of the beat guys went up to Tommy that morning and jokingly asked if he thought he'd still be around when the 3 p.m. deadline passed.

"Why?" Albelin said. "Does the team need some more pucks for practice?"

WEARING NO. 51

Zach Parise showed up for his first professional training camp hoping to earn a spot on New Jersey's Opening Night roster. The Devils issued Parise No. 51, the type of number most rookies wear during their first trip to camp.

He walked in one day and noticed something different. His nameplate was still there, but the number on the back of his jersey had changed. A No. 9 jersey was hanging from his stall.

"They never really tell you, 'You made the team'" Parise said. "[I thought], 'Does that mean I made it or what?'"

But he never asked. "I just kept my mouth shut," Parise said.

Training camp ended and Parise was in the lineup when the Devils opened the 2005–06 season against hotshot rookie Sidney Crosby and the Pittsburgh Penguins. Two seasons later, he led all New Jersey scorers with 31 goals.

He was still waiting for the official word that he'd made the team.

JERSEY JIM

Name the one only Jersey kid who pulled off this hat trick: he played high school hockey in New Jersey; he played his first professional game in a New Jersey sweater; he won the Stanley Cup in New Jersey.

Head down the Garden State Parkway, take it to Exit 91, and you'll find your answer. Jim Dowd, the greatest hockey player to ever come out of Brick, made history when he took his first shift for the Devils during the 1991–92 season.

The legend took root years earlier, when Marshall Johnston called Dowd to tell him New Jersey was selecting him in the eighth round of the 1987 NHL Entry Draft. Dowd was getting ready to run out to a high school graduation party.

"It made the party that much better," Dowd said.

He spent two tours with New Jersey, but no moment touched his heart as dearly as his game-winning goal in Game 2 of the 1995 Stanley Cup Finals. Dowd remembers going to the net, trying to set a screen, when the puck landed on his backhand. A split-second later, he was a hero.

"There's not a better feeling in the world," Dowd said. "It's like hitting a home run in the World Series."

KIIDS AND THEIR FATHERS

Travis Zajac still talks to his father, Tom, after most games. "He coached me until I was thirteen years old," Zajac said.

Zajac and Zach Parise both got started early, both with a little help from their dads. I didn't know Tom, but I played with Zach's dad, J.P., on Long Island. Zach remembers stumbling upon a collection of dad's old hockey photos when he was little.

"All black and white," Parise joked.

Zach learned a lot from his dad. The most important of those lessons? Hustle. Hustle at every practice, hustle at every game.

"He'll be the first to tell you he wasn't the most skilled guy in the league," Parise said. "I guess I got those same genes."

During the 2006–07 hockey season, the two kids made their dads proud, often skating together on the same line.

LOU THE COACH

Lou Lamoriello came out of the dressing room one Monday morning wearing black suit pants and a pair of skates from his days coaching Providence College in the early '80s.

The suit pants were part of Lou's normal wardrobe. The skates were not.

"This is not something I ever had any intention of doing," Lamoriello told reporters that morning.

Larry Robinson eventually got a second chance to coach the Devils, but his second stint lasted just 32 games. Larry resigned two months into the 2005–06 season.

"I feel that I should be able to do more," Robinson told reporters the morning he called it quits. "But I just don't have any more to give. And I think right now my health is more important."

So Lou took the whistle for the first time since that playoff series against Boston back in 1988.

"The most interesting part of the day was when the equipment guy came up to me and said, 'Do you shoot right or left?'" Lamoriello said.

Lou not only took the team to the playoffs. He led them on an improbable come-from-behind run to the Atlantic Division title.

When the season ended, Lou insisted his coaching days were over. He hired Claude Julien to take the reins for the 2006–07 campaign.

But Lou quickly learned to never say, "Never." Looking for a better brand of hockey from his players, Lou fired Julien with three games left in the regular season and took the whistle back.

STAFF PHOTOS

From a few feet away, the photos Lou Lamoriello keeps in a closet in his office look like snapshots of the team standing on the ice after it won the Stanley Cup.

Look closer. There's not a single hockey player in the photos. They're actually shots of the Devils office staff, taken the day after those three New Jersey teams won the Stanley Cup.

"I think it's a significant thing how those people feel," Lamoriello said. "And how important they are, and how sometimes all of us, in any position we're in, really forget how important the little things are."

19

WHERE ARE THEY GOING TO PUT THE SHOT CLOCK?

THERE ARE SO MANY things I love about the Prudential Center. The sightlines are perfect. It is only a few blocks from Penn Station and easily accessible from Routes 78, 21, and 280.

And if you've seen "Chico Eats!" you know I love the concessions.

I think fans have been pleasantly surprised. Before the Devils moved to Newark in 2007, there had been a bunch of shootings. People were scared. I remember someone joking, "Where are they going to put the shot clock—inside the arena or outside the arena?"

We've been pretty fortunate on game nights. Things seem to be getting better. In 2010, the *Star-Ledger* reported that Newark had its first murder-free calendar month in forty-four years. That's progress.

There is one problem with the new building. It's still waiting for a big moment, a baptism that would remind fans of all those great nights at the Meadowlands. I mean, sure, there was the night Marty broke the all-time wins record. But fans—New Jersey fans, especially—measure their hockey team not by individual accomplishments, but by Stanley Cup titles.

The building had plenty of buzz during the team's run to the 2012 Stanley Cup Final. But those moments everyone conjures from the Meadowlands—Marty celebrating in his crease, Scotty circling the ice with the Cup—haven't materialized just yet.

Until that happens, there will be something missing.

THE $100 MILLION MAN

Money made Ilya Kovalchuk an easy target. He signed a 15-year, $100 million contract with the Devils—a deal so expensive, so controversial, the NHL initially rejected it. No Devil had ever been handed that much money. Expectations were sky high.

His first season after signing that megadeal, things got off to a rocky start. Ilya wasn't scoring. To make matters worse, in October, he showed up late for practice. Johnny Mac benched Ilya, creating a rift with his star player.

Personally, I wish Ilya had handled that a little bit differently. I wish Ilya had come out and said, "I'm a leader. I was late for practice. I've got to follow the rules too." But he didn't. And of course, it morphed into so much more.

The low point came during a November game against the Buffalo Sabres. With his team down a goal in a shootout, Ilya skated to center ice, ready to go one-on-one with Buffalo goalie Jhonas Enroth.

Poor Ilya never got a shot off. He lost the puck. The Devils lost the game. I remember he just sagged. He put his head in his hands. To me, that was bottoming out.

But things got better. I guess the most fascinating thing for me was watching him discover the joy of playing defense.

Jacques Lemaire ran a very defensive-minded system. He usually wanted all three forwards back inside the circle. Ilya got used to being a stretch player. He liked to camp out high in the zone, looking for breakout passes so he could blow the zone a little early.

Under Jacques, that changed.

Ilya told me when he stayed in deep, he got the puck deeper in the zone, and that gave him more space. It gave him more room to maneuver. Defensemen could not make their stand at the blue line. They had to retreat to the neutral zone.

If you're making $100 million, you have to ingratiate yourself to teammates and fans by doing the hard things—like playing defense and showing the guys you can be an all-around player. I think that was the best part of Ilya's year.

33 GAMES

John MacLean waited a long time for an opportunity to be a head coach in the National Hockey League. Then on June 17, 2010, his chance arrived. But it lasted just 33 games.

Johnny Mac was an offensive player—one of the best forwards to ever don Jersey colors. He had three 40-goal seasons during his Devils career. I think he thought he could institute a more offensive style in New Jersey.

I don't want to say he had the team playing run n' gun. That wouldn't be fair. But he was definitely encouraging his guys to push the puck out of the neutral zone a little faster.

There were so many issues. The roster had too many new guys. The team wasn't scoring. And when you're not scoring, you have to keep your goals against average down. Johnny

Mac's style was highrisk, high-reward. But the risks weren't paying off.

I think it's safe to say that nobody—nobody—had an overachieving first half of the 2010–11 season. Marty got off to a rough start. Zach Parise got hurt.

For Johnny Mac, nothing went right. I don't think there was anything he could do to stem the tide. The harder he tried, the more things unraveled.

With each loss, the second guessing grew. Maybe he can't coach at this level. Maybe he doesn't know how to get guys out of a rut. All these things that aren't true. Still, the team wasn't winning. I don't know what else Lou Lamoriello could have done. He finally pulled the plug on December 23. The Devils were 9–22–2.

Everybody felt terrible. I really don't believe it was Johnny Mac's coaching. Maybe he should have taken a more conservative approach. Who knows? Maybe it was just poor timing.

Johnny Mac, in my estimation, had no chance to succeed the way the season unfolded. Nobody can say why.

I NEED A DOCTOR

I first met Mike "Doc" Emrick back in the '70s. I was a young goalie; he was a young announcer.

Believe it or not, before he became the voice of the NHL, Doc was calling games in the IHL. When you come from that far down, you're doing more than just broadcasting a game. At that level, you're trying to sell the game. Doc always had that mentality.

I think the greatest compliments I can pay Doc are the same things I would say about a great player. Like Wayne Gretzky or Mario Lemieux, Doc always had that knack for making the people around him better.

He definitely made me better. We spent fourteen years together in that broadcast booth. Our humor slowly began to mesh. We became such good friends away from the rink. I was not surprised one bit when he won an Emmy Award in 2011.

The Devils have had some big names walk through that dressing room over the years—Martin Brodeur, Scott Stevens, Ken Daneyko, Scott Niedermayer. Doc belongs in that same class, alongside all those legendary Devils.

Of course, you will never get him to admit that. That guy is humble, much more humble and shy than he appears on air. And that's what keeps him grounded. He always makes sure to present himself, the team and the game in the right light.

It was sad the day we talked and he told me he was leaving our booth. Doc decided to cut back on his schedule. He stepped away from the Devils gig but continues to call games for NBC.

CHICO EATS!

I've eaten hot dogs, burritos, nachos, and soft-serve ice cream. I've eaten inside the arena and outside the arena. I've eaten hummus. I've eaten sushi.

Fans seem to get a kick out of "Chico Eats!" a segment we've run on Devils broadcasts for the past few years. I wish I could take credit for the idea, but "Chico Eats!" was the brainchild of our producer Roland Dratch. He thought it would be funny if I tried something from a different concession stand each game. When we ran out of concessions, I started visiting restaurants near the rink in Newark.

I don't think there are better concession stands anywhere in the NHL. There is not a bad morsel of food in that building.

Trust me. I've tried most of it.

ZACH ATTACK

You never know if a young player is going to pan out. But Zach Parise certainly did.

After stealing him with the No. 17 pick in the 2003 NHL Entry Draft, the Devils have watched Zach blossom into a wonderful hockey player. He had a run of four straight 30-goal seasons for the Devils until a knee injury bumped him from all but 13 games during the 2010–11 season.

One of the biggest goals of his hockey career came on one of the biggest stages. Zach was on the ice as the seconds ticked down during the 2010 Olympics gold medal game. With the United States trailing Canada 2–1, hoping for another miracle, Zach put the puck in the net to tie it, stunning the Vancouver crowd.

Canada would win the game on a Sidney Crosby goal in overtime—a heartbreaker for the Americans—yet Zach proved his worth as a clutch forward.

HALL OF FAMERS

Slowly but surely, people who spent part of their career in New Jersey are cracking the wall, finding a way inside the Hockey Hall of Fame in Toronto.

In 2011, two forwards with Devils ties were joining the ranks. Joe Nieuwendyk, a gritty veteran who logged minutes for the '03 Cup victors, was scheduled to join Doug Gilmour, a scoring machine who had seven goals and 15 assists during a 20-game run with New Jersey in '97. A few other players—

Slava Fetisov and Igor Larionov—are also in there, although like Nieuwendyk and Gilmour, some of their best work was done with other teams.

Lou Lamoriello, the architect of those three Cup wins, went into the Hall as a builder in '09. It's hard to argue with that.

And of course, there is the captain of those Cup winners—Scotty Stevens. Scotty was elected in '07, the first year he was eligible. I remember watching Scotty after he threw some of those big hits. He would skate to the bench and stare off into space.

I finally asked him what was going through his mind during those moments.

Who's going to come after me now?

Jeez, that felt good.

He said, "No, you know, I knew that was my game. That was the choices that they made and that was the choice I had to make to finish the check as hard as I could. A couple of times, I felt a little bit bad that the results turned out the way it did."

I think that's what made Scotty so special. He could separate it. He knew that if you hit someone hard, you were discouraging that player from using his skill in the same manner the next trip down the ice.

He's not cocky. There's no bravado to his personality. He's just a really down-to-earth, humble guy.

That's what makes him so interesting. Nice guy, but he's going to go down as one of the greatest hitters the game has ever seen.

20

"I STILL GET CHILLS"

WHEN THE DEVILS returned to the Stanley Cup Finals in 2012, a young kid named Adam Henrique helped them get there. Most Devils fans remember the overtime goal Adam scored against the Rangers in Game 6, dropping the curtain on the series and catapulting New Jersey into the next round.

But most people don't know Adam almost didn't make it out there for overtime after stopping a shot during the third period.

"I blocked a slapper right in the groin," Henrique said. "Oh, did it hurt."

Between periods, New Jersey's staff members examined Adam. They instructed him to sit down hard a few times in his locker stall. When he was able to complete that exercise without much pain, he was permitted to return to the ice.

It didn't take long. Adam tapped in the game-winner just 63 seconds into the extra session. The celebration began.

"When we went in the corner and we started to celebrate, I got lightheaded," said Henrique's former teammate Zach

Parise. "I was lightheaded. I couldn't think. I was in La La Land."

Looking back, Adam confessed he does wonder what would have happened if things played out differently.

"I've often thought if I had been injured more seriously, I probably wouldn't have been out there for the first shift," Henrique said. "It's funny how fate goes."

"But I still get chills . . . It's still the most incredible moment of my career."

STANDING UP FOR A TEAMMATE

Ilya Kovalchuk took a lot of heat for fleeing New Jersey only three years after signing a $100 million contract. It's tough to blame fans for being angry.

But he did have some great moments while he was here. And to hear Zach Parise tell it, he really was a terrific teammate.

Zach reminded me about a regular season game the Devils played against the Flyers in 2012. When those two teams face off, things tend to get a little crazy. This time was no different.

In the third period, with the Devils up 6–2, the game took an ugly turn. Philadelphia forward Zac Rinaldo kicked Zach's foot out from under him, dropping him to the ice. It was a dirty play. And Kovy took notice.

Kovy made a bee line for Rinaldo and began throwing punches. As officials tried to pry players from both teams away from each other, Kovy got involved with Philadelphia's Brayden Schenn. Both players removed their gloves. In the fight that followed, Kovy dropped Schenn with a thunderous right hand.

"I remember thinking, 'Kovy really cares,'" Parise said. "Kovy cared more than people realized about winning and being a good team guy."

That postseason, Zach tried to return the favor.

"Somebody ran Kovy," Parise said. "And I stepped in and tried to sort of do the same thing. I didn't fight the guy, but I stepped in and tried to stand up for Kovy."

It's too bad for Devils fans. Kovy and Zach were made to play together. But Kovy went home to Russia. And Zach returned to Minnesota. Their departures forced the Devils to move on without one of the best combinations the franchise has ever had.

"I CAN'T SAY IT DIDN'T HURT"

The hardest part was the phone call. Zach Parise dialed Lou Lamoriello's office to let him know he had made his decision. After seven seasons in New Jersey, Zach was signing with Minnesota.

Marie Carnevale, Lou's longtime executive assistant, picked up the phone when Zach called.

"As tough as it was telling Lou," Parise said, "what was really tough was when Marie came on. We talked for a few moments. Marie knew that I had made a decision. She was so professional. She didn't ask. That was when I kind of started to choke up."

Zach has plenty of great memories from his time here in Jersey. He remembers that when the team returned from Los Angeles after losing the 2012 Stanley Cup Final, fans waited outside the Prudential Center for the players to arrive back home. As Zach got off the bus, fans chanted, "Come back Zach! Come back Zach!"

"That got me very, very emotional," Parise said.

Things changed after he left. During Zach's first trip back in a Minnesota Wild sweater, Devils fans let him have it. I asked Zach what it was like hearing those boos from the same fans that wanted him back. Zach told me, "I can't say it didn't hurt."

"I understand why they would be disappointed," Parise said. "But I don't think they understand all that was pulling at me and the fact that it was the toughest decision of my life."

Zach said the Devils made a very generous offer when he was a free agent. In the end, he just wanted to go home.

Maybe this was a case of divine intervention. Less than two years after signing with Minnesota, Zach's father J.P. was diagnosed with lung cancer. As J.P. battled the disease from his Minnesota home, Zach was never far away.

J.P. died in 2015. He was seventy-three.

LIFE ON THE FARM

Adam Henrique has never been much of a morning person. Growing up on a tobacco farm, Adam remembers his dad, Joe, used to hop out of bed by 4 a.m.

"A good time to start for me is nine o'clock," Henrique joked.

Still, he learned a lot of lessons growing up on that Burford, Ontario, farm with his brothers.

"I was the grunt guy," Henrique said. "I would just do the odd jobs, whatever Dad or [my brother] Mike would ask me to do."

His brother used a tractor to cut the top part of the tobacco plants. But the tractor could not clip the lower leaves. Those leaves needed to be trimmed by hand.

One summer, Adam was assigned to sit on a chair and clip those lower leaves—row by row, hour after hour. The tar from the tobacco plants would spill all over his hands.

"My hands got dirty and gritty," Henrique said. "I like to think that's maybe why my game's a little dirty and gritty."

He got to know many of the Mexican immigrants who worked on his family's farm. Even as a kid, he admired the way they carried themselves.

"I was so impressed by those guys," Henrique said. "They got up early, never complained. I just admired their work ethic. Everywhere I looked, I saw the example of hard work. And so they were good role models for me.

"One thing I learned from the farm was that everybody had a role and everybody needed to get their job done and everybody needed a coach. When things were working well on the farm, it was a well-oiled machine."

Just like hockey.

THE GREATEST

One of the great pastimes while talking sports is when people discuss who is the greatest. The answer is always subjective. That's what makes it fun.

Let me discuss one sports figure where I don't believe there can be any debate. His name is Marty Brodeur.

For over fifty years, I have closely observed or played against every NHL goalie who has ever put on the pads. And I believe that Marty is the greatest regular season goalie of all time, bar none.

Marty's regular season statistics are staggering (691 wins, 125 shutouts, a lifetime 2.24 goals against average). Many times at the morning skate, opposing goalies would call me over and ask questions like:

How can Marty play that stand-up style and never get beaten low to the corners or be vulnerable through the legs?

How can he challenge the shooters by coming out of the crease as often as he does and never get beaten back to the post?

How can he venture from the crease to chase pucks, and yet never get trapped away from the net for an easy tap-in?

If Marty played the puck, let's say, 15,000 times in his career, I can't remember more than ten times he made a bad play with the puck which led to a direct goal.

Opposing goalies also asked me if he got along with his backups. Chris Terreri was—and still is—one of his closest former goalie teammates. The other goalies that came to New Jersey to be his backup were treated with respect, but were never what you would call close friends.

Marty told me that although he respected and cared about his goaltending partners, he wanted to play almost every single night. I believe that Marty's awareness that his calling in life was not only to play goal, but to become one of the all-time greats, limited his desire to become too close to the other goalies.

Jacques Plante, Kenny Dryden, Glenn Hall, Patrick Roy, and others were caught in the same predicament. With goaltending, you need to have the attitude that there's only one net. If it's either the other goalie or you to carry the team, you have to eliminate the competition. Both Marty and his teammates realized that was the situation.

I get to say this, but I know everyone feels it: Marty, we miss you. I never once got tired of watching you play, hearing your interviews, and observing how much you enjoyed the privileged life of an NHL goalie. You never took it for granted. And I know you never took your teammates and fans for granted either.

I really wish there was another Martin Brodeur coming along, but you set the bar so high, my friend. I guarantee that will never happen.

LOU LEAVES

No one thought it would ever happen. No one imagined that one day Lou Lamoriello would voluntarily leave after twenty-seven seasons with the New Jersey Devils. But in 2015, he did. Lou took over as general manager of the Toronto Maple Leafs.

"It wasn't easy," Lamoriello said at his introductory press conference in Toronto. "I've always said, 'Anything easy isn't worth it.' . . . This is a challenge and I'm extremely excited about it."

So how did it get to this point? How did the architect of all those great Devils teams wind up moving into a lesser role in New Jersey before eventually bolting for Toronto?

You can trace it back to 2012, when the Devils made that memorable run to the Stanley Cup Final. As well as that team played, the run helped mask a lot of the issues that were bubbling beneath the surface.

The team was starting to get older. The style of play they used to win three Stanley Cups was no longer as effective. Even the great Marty Brodeur was starting to show signs of wear.

Lou used to tell me, "Chico, we're never in a rebuilding process. We're always going for it." That attitude worked for a long time. But times were changing.

I believe there were two reasons why Lou eventually ran into trouble with the Devils.

1. New Jersey's seemingly endless pool of minor league talent—a system that produced everyone from Patrik Elias to Zach Parise—had finally run dry. All those blue chip prospects Lou found earlier in his career were suddenly missing.

2. Lou tried desperately to keep on winning. In order to accomplish that, he signed a lot of older free agents. Quite honestly, not many of those aging players made much of an impact.

After that 2012 series, things took a turn for the worse. His lowest moment was probably when he wasn't able to bring back Kovy or re-sign Zach. In the past, he might have been able to convince both men to stay.

I believe the change was good for Lou. He spent all those decades with all these powerful people working under him. Now he had powerful people that were equals. He always believed in the team concept and now he was being asked to be part of a team himself.

Lou needed to push the refresh button. I think that occurred when he went up to Toronto.

RAY OF LIGHT

Back when Ray Shero was playing college hockey at St. Lawrence, his father, Fred, was calling Devils games on the radio following his Hall of Fame coaching career. Ray remembers coming home around the holidays and attending games with his dad.

One game, Fred even interviewed his son during the broadcast.

Three decades later—in the spring of 2015—Fred's son was named general manager of the Devils. It was a stunning announcement for a franchise that had hired only one GM during the previous twenty-eight years—Lou Lamoriello. Even stranger: Lou would be staying on board as president of hockey operations.

Ray, who had built a Stanley-Cup winning squad as general manager of the Pittsburgh Penguins, was willing to come to New Jersey, but he needed to establish that he did things differently than Lou. He needed to know he would have the autonomy to implement his own ideas.

Lou agreed. Slowly but surely, Ray began to make a few tweaks.

He instituted a father's trip, allowing dads to accompany their sons on the road. He loosened the reins on the team's facial hair policy. He had the team stay in New York the night before games against the Rangers and Islanders.

"I made it clear to Lou I wasn't trying to disrespect him," Shero said. "I just do things differently."

One of the biggest tweaks was the way the Devils approached the game. Ray didn't want players sitting back. He wanted them to pounce.

The Devils only had 84 points during Ray's first season as GM. But the team was fun to watch. And after missing the playoffs during four of the previous five seasons, things seemed as if they were headed in the right direction.

30 x 2 =

Even though hockey is a team game, it's fun to watch young guys chase individual milestones. And at the end of the 2015–16 season, the Devils had two players inching close to the first 30-goal seasons of their career.

With one game to play, Kyle Palmieri had 29 goals. Adam Henrique had 28.

All season long, these two young players pushed each other. Their friendly rivalry and dueling quests to lead New Jersey in scoring would bring out the best in both of them.

Game No. 82 was in New Jersey against former Devils general manager Lou Lamoriello's Maple Leafs.

"It was on Hockey Night in Canada in Toronto," Henrique said. "So I knew all my family and friends would be watching."

In the second period of a 1–1 game, Henrique was lingering near the right side of the net when teammate Adam Larsson unleashed a slap shot from the blue line. Toronto goalie Garret Sparks made the initial stop, but the rebound took a wild bounce, hopping up off the ice and into Henrique's body before it landed in the back of the net.

Twenty-nine.

Less than ten minutes later, he zoomed up the right side and tapped another puck past Sparks—this time with his stick.

Thirty.

"I was beyond excited," Henrique said. "I took a deep breath and said to myself, 'Wow. I just reached the 30-goal plateau.' That's a big milestone for a player like me."

After the game, Adam called home. His mother Teresa—the Henrique family's hockey guru, the one who always asks her son if he is getting enough sleep or having trouble with his game—was happy to hear from him.

"The call home to mom and dad was really sweet," Henrique said.

But the story gets even better. With less than three minutes to play in the game and the Devils leading 3–1, Toronto pulled its goalie. Palmieri—the other guy chasing that 30-goal plateau—hit an empty net from mid-ice.

For the first time in four years, the Devils had a pair of 30-goal scorers. The last time that happened, when Henrique's former linemates Ilya Kovaluchuk and Zach Parise did it, New Jersey went all the way to the Stanley Cup Final.

END OF AN ERA

It was odd watching the final seconds bleed off the clock on April 13, 2014. These would turn out to be the final seconds of Martin Brodeur's 21 seasons as a Devils goalie.

Cory Schneider was ready to take over as the go-to guy for New Jersey. But Marty still had some goals he desperately wanted to reach.

At times during that last season, Marty looked bored sitting on the bench. He knew he was very close to becoming Cory's backup. The situation was becoming uncomfortable. Everyone hated the white elephant in the room, but until the end of the season, that big animal wasn't going anywhere.

And then one April afternoon against the Boston Bruins, the illustrious Devils career of Martin Brodeur came to an end. Not that anyone was 100 percent sure it had ended. I felt for the die-hard Devils fans that were there. They didn't know how to react when the game ended. Was it appropriate to give the raucous ovation that a player like Marty deserved? Or would Marty feel disrespected, as if they were saying, "This is it, Marty. It's time to move on."

Marty's last game just sort of drifted away into hockey history, with everyone wondering, "What really just happened here?"

Almost two years later—after Brodeur's brief stint as a back-up goalie with the St. Louis Blues—fans would finally get to celebrate his career. The Devils unveiled a statue and sent No. 30 up to the Prudential Center rafters.

The retirement celebration night was vintage Brodeur and his fans. There was a strong, loving, appreciative bond that permeated the festivities, but it wasn't over the top.

When the Devils legend started to speak, he was drowned out by chants of "Mar-ty, Mar-ty." He backed away from the podium, raised his right hand, and acknowledged this out-pouring of love from his fans.

"I value and I cherish the relationship I had with you guys," Brodeur said. "I'll remember it forever. Thanks for all the memories. Thank you for all the 'Marty's better' chants. And keep being one of the best fan bases in the NHL."

I couldn't put it any better myself.